Holding Down the Fort

D0556161

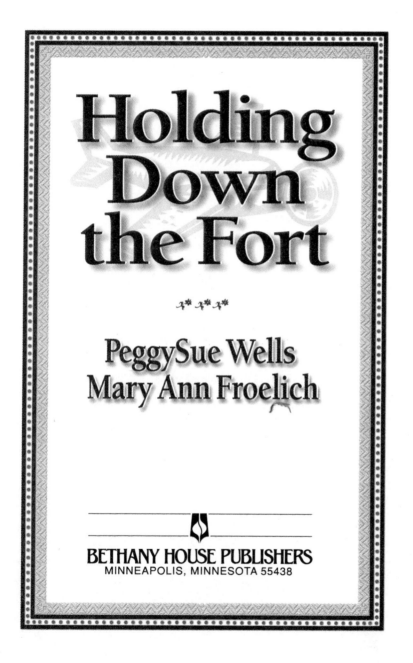

Holding Down the Fort

PeggySue Wells
Mary Ann Froelich

BETHANY HOUSE PUBLISHERS
MINNEAPOLIS, MINNESOTA 55438

Holding Down the Fort
Copyright © 1998
PeggySue Wells & Mary Ann Froehlich

Cover design by Terry Dugan

Published by Bethany House Publishers
A Ministry of Bethany Fellowship International
11400 Hampshire Avenue South
Minneapolis, Minnesota 55438
www.bethanyhouse.com

Printed in the United States of America by
Bethany Press International, Minneapolis, Minnesota 55438

Library of Congress Cataloging-in-Publication Data

CIP data applied for

ISBN 0–7642–2079–9   CIP

To

Keith, AmyRose, Leilani, Holly,
Josiah, Estee, Hannah,
and our coming blessing

who love me unconditionally.

PSW

———

To

John, Janelle, Natalie, and Cameron—
who have taught me about the travel lifestyle,

and my parents—
who so readily lend an extra pair of hands

all of whom I dearly love.

MAF

PEGGYSUE WELLS is a wife, mother, homemaker, teacher, childbirth educator, graphic artist, editor, and freelance writer. Her writing credits include many local and national by-lines. Her husband travels frequently in marketing. They make their home with their six children in Indiana.

MARY ANN FROEHLICH is a board certified music therapist, Suzuki music teacher, and the author of several books. Her education includes a doctorate in music education from the University of Southern California and a master's degree in pastoral care from Fuller Theological Seminary. Her husband travels weekly as vice-president of HCIA. They make their home in California with their three children.

Acknowledgments

Many heartfelt thanks to:

All the contributors whose names are found throughout this book, and to those who chose to remain anonymous. You are the heart of the message found in these humble pages.

Pat Palau for her consistent and patient support and encouragement.

Ann Parrish, who believed in our project, and our friends at Bethany House Publishers who have brought the vision to completion.

Mary Ann Froehlich, who believes in me. You have been the wind under my wings.

Contents

Foreword

Years ago the Industrial Revolution effectively removed fathers from the home and the core of family life, leaving society with the popular "Bumstead" image of the family man. A second revolution is currently shaking the foundation of the family as we know it. On October 20, 1997, *USA Today's* cover story reported 42.9 million people travel for business, a 21 percent increase since 1991. Today's increased business travel demands have created a generation of frequently absent spouses and parents.

What will be the impact on this generation of marriages? What will be the impact on the children—our children—raised with a frequently absent parent?

A navy chaplain once told me, "I've seen wives of sailors jump into the water in a futile, senseless effort to follow their husband's boat as it pulls away from the dock." Such was their state of panic over their husband leaving them alone again.

Frequent travel of business people, as well as military personnel, turns many people into part-time absentee spouses and parents. The toll on family life is often severe. Equally costly is the recurrent unavailability of the addict and the so-called workaholic. Our society exhibits concern for children from "broken" homes due to divorce or abandonment. But aren't children with a frequently absent parent also at risk? How can we help them?

The authors of this book have gathered honest stories portraying the problems, pain, and triumphs of families with a "gone again" member. The stories include the perspective of spouses, parents, and children; the traveler as well as the ones left at home.

The accounts are realistic—not always pleasant—sometimes appearing downright impossible. Living as a part-time single parent is tough. Being away from home can be tedious. Not all the difficulties result from the family member's absence; some stem from that person's temporary presence. Families grieve when the travelers leave, then struggle to assimilate them again into the family circle accustomed to functioning without them.

Thankfully, the interviewees do more than divulge their struggles; they also share their solutions. The answers are many, and they are practical. In this book you will find answers that work.

I trust you will discover in your situation, like theirs, that God's grace can help us not merely survive, but triumph.

—Dr. Charles M. Sell
    Professor of Educational Ministries
    at Trinity Evangelical Divinity School
    Director of the Center for Family Life
    Author of *Power Dads*

Introduction

"Is John in town this week?" my friend asks.

"No, he's in Texas. Is Keith in town?" I respond.

"No . . . and this is a ten-day trip. Those are the worst. How would you like to come over for pizza tonight?"

Our conversations often start like this. PeggySue and I both have husbands who travel. Keith is in manufacturing management and frequently travels to market the product. My husband, John, has his own health care consulting business and gives presentations all over the United States. Travel is a given in their professions. In our global age spouses fly across the country as commonly as our fathers commuted half an hour to work.

PeggySue and I are not alone. Many couples today are seeking to raise committed families around traveling obstacles. I look at a young mother whose husband is traveling to Africa for three weeks, and I feel like the lucky one. John is only on the East Coast for four days.

Well-meaning friends ask, "Can't your husband find another job? It can't be healthy for your family to have him gone so often." These comments break our hearts. It is not realistic that our husbands find jobs in their fields without travel. Yet no one wants to talk about it. To pretend the issues are not there only makes it harder to support each other.

It is realistic to find the best and most biblical way to cope with the challenge. John and I have three children, while PeggySue and Keith have six. We wrote this book for us, desiring to know how other families succeed at this task. This is not a theoretical book or a how-to book. We present these families' stories without judgment or embellishment. Each person's experience is unique. You, the reader, will evaluate the relevancy for your own life.

Our book project grew as we considered the different circumstances that cause a spouse to hold down the fort alone. Our personal experience was short-term travel, but others experienced an absent spouse due to a military career, workaholism, even addictions and imprisonment. We included these situations, as well as women who travel.

Each chapter focuses on a common reason for a traveling, or frequently absent, spouse. Chapters open with a key Scripture verse and a vignette (a slice of life, so to speak). Chapters highlight a family new to the lifestyle, one who has been doing this for a while, and a family who is veteran to this situation. Strategies gleaned from these families are summarized at the end of each chapter to help readers immediately apply successful principles in their own lives.

Since this book was a project years in the making, we learned that the one constant in the travel life is *change*. Unpredictability rules. Updated epilogues are included, even our own, to illustrate this point.

We want to bring hope, confidence, and encouragement to others who share our vision to nurture loving and healthy families despite our culture's demands. Our biblical calling is to be on the battlefield of the tough issues. Would our first choice be that our husbands did not travel? Absolutely yes! But more important is our choice to follow our Lord and run the race before us.

CHAPTER ONE

Mary Ann's Story

If I rise on the wings of the dawn, if I settle on the far side of the sea,
even there your hand will guide me, your right hand will hold me fast.

—*Psalm 139:9–10*

W HY DOES DADDY TAKE HIS SUITCASE TO WORK?" my toddler
asks.

That suitcase—it sits in the corner of our bedroom, a constant reminder that our lives are different. We don't even put it away anymore
because in a few days it will be packed for another trip. That suitcase—
I can make peace with it, or I can see it as a rival. That suitcase has
changed my life.

I never chose to be a single parent of three young children—yet
in reality that is what I am most weeks out of the year.

In twenty years of marriage, John and I have never been strangers
to demanding schedules. In his previous job as a hospital administra-
tor, John often left for work at 5:00 A.M. and returned after board
meetings at 11:00 P.M. Exhaustion was the norm.

Eight years ago John made one of the most difficult decisions of
his life. The pressures of his job had become too intense, and he left
the security of salary and position to start his own health care consulting business. We knew the first year would be the most difficult.
He rented a back corner desk in a friend's office and typed his own
correspondence because he couldn't afford a secretary. Often there
wasn't enough money to go to the market, so in addition to being a
full-time mom, I taught piano and wrote.

A hard worker and talented businessman, John persevered to build a successful company. Today he has his own office, a wonderful staff, and a fine reputation in the health care field. John consults with hospitals all over the country. But the more clients he gains, the more he travels.

I am proud of John, and I support him. It's a privilege for a wife to share her husband's vision and help him attain his dreams. Yet holding down the fort alone is a struggle. I have struggled emotionally with depression and loneliness. I have struggled physically with exhaustion. But in that dark place of struggle is where God builds strength of character and nurtures perseverance.

One of my favorite passages of Scripture says,

> Jesus made his disciples get into the boat and go on ahead of him to Bethsaida, while he dismissed the crowd. After leaving them, he went up on a mountainside to pray. When evening came, the boat was in the middle of the lake, and he was alone on land. He saw the disciples straining at the oars, because the wind was against them. About the fourth watch of the night he went out to them, walking on the lake. He was about to pass by them, but when they saw him walking on the lake, they thought he was a ghost. They cried out, because they all saw him and were terrified.
>
> Immediately he spoke to them and said, "Take courage! It is I. Don't be afraid." Then he climbed into the boat with them, and the wind died down. They were completely amazed.
>
> —Mark 6:45–51

Jesus watched His followers struggling. He could have immediately calmed the wind from the shore. But Jesus waited. Then He went out to be with them in their struggle. His relationship with the disciples came first; it was important that they trust Him in the midst of the storm. In essence He said, "Be courageous. You are not alone. I am here with you. There is nothing to fear." *Then* He solved the problem.

This is the real miracle. God does not immediately solve our problems like a fairy godmother with a magic wand. He comes to be with us in the midst of our struggles, comforting us with His presence. Our relationship with Him is more important than the solution to our problems.

WAS I READY FOR THIS?

In some ways I was well-prepared for this challenge. Raised as an only child, I learned to enjoy being alone and occupy myself easily. I welcome solitude, the peace and refreshment it brings, as well as concentrated time for projects. I doubt that my own three children would easily adapt to a traveling spouse because they thrive on family interaction.

John and I have been friends since we met during college. Some find our relationship unusual. I liked John when I met him because he was bright, he made me laugh, he made me think, he challenged and interested me. John respects my quiet, independent nature and gives me the space I need. I do the same for him. Though not a model for other relationships, it is the balance that works for us. Varying temperaments and marriage roles affect a couple's adaptability to travel.

In other ways I was ill-prepared for this high-stress travel lifestyle. I had no role models. My dad came home every night at 5:00 P.M. for dinner. He worshiped my mom. My father never did laundry or cooked in the kitchen. My mother, a strong and talented woman, never took the trash out, washed her car, or put gas in it. Their well-defined system was no reflection of stereotyped roles of superiority/inferiority. It was a system of caring and love. Then I married John, the hard-driving career man who simply wasn't home much. I soon learned that if I needed something done, I'd better figure out how to do it myself.

John and I have a solid but challenging marriage. We are 100 percent committed to God, each other, and our family. This commitment has been our stability through difficult times. We have had to work at the travel lifestyle just as we have grappled with other issues. Here are some practical ideas that have eased our way.

HOW JOHN HELPS US

Owning his own business, John can never send someone else on a trip. If John does not go, we don't eat that month. Our children know that traveling is what Daddy does to support us, but they also know that they come first. When he is at work, John is 100 percent at work. When John is with his children, he is 100 percent with them.

- When traveling, John calls every night to talk with each child and hear about the day.
- John plans trips around special events for the children. He may need to travel for a week, but he can also take three days off to go on a school camp-out or take the children skiing. To avoid becoming victims of his schedule, we plan our calendars together.
- John is home on the weekends whenever possible.
- He makes every effort to participate in family traditions and activities. Traditions bond our family and create a sense of belonging.
- He carries a copy of his eldest daughter's math book in his suitcase to help nightly with homework by phone. This has become a bond between them. The phone bills are costly but worth it.
- John sets up safeguards against temptations that could destroy our marriage. John takes female business associates out to dinner only when accompanied by the husband or other co-workers. He shocked me some time ago when he told me women have propositioned him when he travels. "It's normal in business, and some women use it to their advantage," he said. "It doesn't matter what men look like or who they are—women will approach them."
- John makes his homecoming a joyous time with presents representative of the city he has visited. The longer and farther the trip, the bigger the presents. He also takes us out to dinner when he arrives home.

HOW WE HELP JOHN

I have never thought for a minute that John leads the glamorous life while I'm stuck at home.

- The most important thing we do for John is pray for him. Constant plane flights, waiting in airports, lonely hotel rooms, pressured meetings, and exhausting time changes make for a miserable week.

His comment about temptations awakened me to the fact that he is human. He can be lonely and tempted.

- We try to bring a sense of home to John by hiding cards, pictures, and gifts in his luggage with tags labeled OPEN DAY #1, DAY #2, etc.
- I do not make personal plans when John is home. Understandably, he wants me to be with him. We guard Saturday as our family time and often leave for the day on adventures with the kids.
- I try not to have chores or projects waiting for John so he can spend all his free time with the children.

HOW I HELP MYSELF

I must take care of myself spiritually, or rather let God take care of me. Complete reliance upon God is the key to survival. Keeping focused on Jesus Christ as my constant companion and rescuer and being rooted in Scripture daily are critical. I cannot depend on my husband, or any other human being, to be my savior. Husbands will not survive that kind of pressure in addition to their work stresses.

- I choose to use the travel lifestyle as an opportunity for God to build character rather than allowing the enemy to use it to destroy my family. In every mature believer's life, I believe God brings two experiences to develop godly character: (1) a person who requires unconditional love, acceptance, and forgiveness from us. Only then can we truly understand God's love for us and His chain of mercy; and (2) a situation where we must completely depend on God with no options. In today's society, keeping families intact is a battle.
- I need to pace myself through the day because I will need energy at the end of the day to cook dinner, wash dishes, help with homework and bedtime reading, give baths, and put three kids to bed. I believe talking and praying with the children at night is the most important part of the day, so I do not want to sacrifice that. And no one comes home to help carry the load.

- I need to care for myself physically so I am not susceptible to illness. Needing to lower my expectations about what I can accomplish, I cannot become overcommitted outside the home, especially with evening activities.
- Hobbies and projects fill my lonely hours, provide a healthy diversion, keep me from becoming too driven, and help me develop my own interests. No woman should seek her identity from her husband's life. My music and writing have been great comforts, channeling heartache and energy toward a constructive purpose.

HOW WE HELP OUR CHILDREN

When one spouse is the hurricane, the other spouse needs to be the anchor. A godly counselor described to me his nightmare childhood with an alcoholic and abusive father. He concluded, "But through it all, my mom was always there . . . she simply was there and that security upheld me through a lot of pain."

I cannot give my children a perfect life, but I can "simply always be there." Mothers play a powerful role.

- I try not to compare our family with others who have a more "normal" schedule.
- Routine becomes essential. Life cannot fall apart because Daddy is not here. Maintaining holiday traditions, as well as a regular dinner hour, prevent the television and fast food from becoming a "Daddy substitute."
- Planning special activities for the children with their friends when John is gone helps the time pass more quickly.
- Attitude and choice of words are critical. I can pass to my children resentment, anger, and bitterness or compassion and love. My attitude can convey, "Daddy isn't here and he doesn't care," or "Daddy misses us and wishes he were here." To keep him part of daily activities, I like to talk about John as if he were present: "Daddy would like that" or "Wait until you tell Daddy."
- Understanding that our children can become fearful at night when

Daddy is out of town, I sometimes allow them to sleep in our bedroom. We call these times our "special camp-outs." The children don't know I am often as afraid as they are.

- I look to God for the strength to be a strong, godly role model whom my children see trusting God daily.

HOW FAMILY AND FRIENDS HELP

Next to dependence on God, the most important lifeline is a support system of friends, ideally other women with traveling husbands. Sometimes friends send a card when I am most discouraged, call when I am most lonely, or offer help when I am most exhausted.

- When friends offer to help, I let them. Friends are God's tangible arms around me. My coauthor, PeggySue, knows my pain. I have nicknamed her my "soup friend" because she has brought me the most delicious pots of soup on difficult days. She knows that I feed the children what they enjoy but don't take time to eat well myself. One single mom calls to have heart-to-heart talks during the empty late-night hours when my friends with husbands at home aren't available. One night another friend came to sit with me while I gave the kids their baths. There is so much to do alone that a little company and laughter eases the load.
- My dear parents, who live across the state, visit when John is gone. It is wonderful to have another pair of hands, another driver, another cook, etc. Their visits are special treats for our children and for me.
- I can either wallow in the "Poor me, I'm a victim" syndrome (and I have had lots of good pity parties), or I can minister to others who struggle with the same pain. Reaching out contributes to my own healing. There are plenty of other single moms out there who need a lifeline. I enjoy planning luncheons for my friends when John is out of town. It keeps me busy through the week, nourishes me with fellowship, and provides leftovers for dinner. So if I'm feeling blue, I give myself a party!

- I must nurture friendships. I cannot wait for someone to reach out to me first because I will drown while I am waiting. Women must beware of dependence on male friendships, as such friends can become surrogate husbands and even lovers. Too many of my lonely friends have crossed the line before realizing it was too late to save their marriages.
- I cannot take offense when friends, especially ones with husbands at home, do not call. They are not callous or uncaring. They truly have no idea what I am going through.

THE STRUGGLE CONTINUES

I would not be honest if I left you thinking that we have mastered this lifestyle. We have struggled in the past and still do today. This is a survival lifestyle that pushes any marriage to the edge. And no one wants to merely survive.

These survival strategies sound great on paper, but this lifestyle leaves no room for error or unexpected crises. Social gatherings sound fun, but what if Mom has the flu all week? Hobbies are healthy, but by the end of the day we are too exhausted to concentrate. We collapse into bed, longing for a companion to comfort us. If we fought just before our husband left on his trip, we worry about a plane crash and think, "What if this is the time he doesn't come back?" What about those sounds in the middle of the night that scare us, no matter how many Scripture passages we've read about God's protection? We aspire to the ideal, but we live in reality.

How do partners work out conflicts when one partner is often gone? Of course John and I deal with other issues in our marriage besides his travel. Counselors say the first thing struggling couples need to do is spend time together talking. So what do we do? We are forced to put our issues on hold, and that is not healthy. I am thankful to be married to a man who is as committed as I am to this marriage. Our commitment has been the glue that has held us together through many tough spots. John and I have had to diligently work on our communication skills.

What kind of picture are we portraying to our children about marriage? I want to be a strong, godly woman who functions well independently, but I do not want to teach my girls that women should not depend on their husbands or fathers. It is a fine line. What messages is our son receiving? I do not want to fall apart when John is gone, but I also need to be honest with myself and my children. Depression, loneliness, and fear are realities in this lifestyle. It is unhealthy to pretend them away. As a children's therapist, I know that children need to grieve and talk about their pain in order to cope with it. Otherwise they will carry this baggage into adulthood, where it is more difficult to work through.

It is painful for any mother to hear that her children are hurting and she cannot stop it. Travel is a different kind of loss, similar to death or divorce. Even divorced dads see their kids every weekend. My tendency is to keep our kids so busy that they don't miss their dad. But I have come to realize that we need to miss Dad. We can't wallow in it, but we can be honest. One of our daughters began crying nightly and having stomachaches in her father's absence. John and I strategized a plan—e-mail. Our daughter felt better once she could contact her dad via e-mail whenever she desired.

How do we best prepare our children for Dad's absence? John has been reluctant to tell the children about upcoming trips because he hates to hear their response. Be we have learned that children should be prepared, not surprised. Though it is difficult, John is learning to talk to the children about his traveling. Our son CJ once told me, "I wish I had two daddies. I need one daddy to go to work and one daddy to stay home to play with me."

Young children are especially vulnerable because they have not developed adult time concepts. Babies are relatively unaffected. Older children and teens understand when Dad will be home. But the young child doesn't understand. A week is a long time to a toddler. "Is today when Daddy comes home?" "How many tomorrows until he comes?" During one of his dad's trips, CJ (then three) proudly wrote letters to Daddy on Monday morning and left them by the front door to be opened that night. John was not coming home until late Friday night.

Every day CJ waited for his dad to come get his mail. It broke my heart. Finally Daddy came home to those waiting letters. I hurt for John that he misses these daily tokens of affection. I hurt for my children. *I hurt.*

How do we convey the image of an ever-present heavenly Father when their earthly father is often not around? My greatest fear is that our children will see God as a good father but an often absent father. Will His daily presence be a reality for them? I also need to guard my own emotional response. My children are a great source of love and affection for me, and yet I need to be careful not to emotionally substitute them for their dad. Someday the children will be gone.

How do we find balance in this crazy lifestyle? John could work seven days a week, eighteen hours a day, and still fall behind. In past years before leaving on a trip, John pushed himself to finish presentations and meet deadlines, often burning the midnight oil. Upon his return he was exhausted from time changes and swamped with new developments at work. The trip may have lasted a week, but we lost him for two weeks. Neither of us ever got recharged. This year John has deliberately worked at pacing himself. When he doesn't drive himself so hard, life is easier for all of us.

So are we travel widows of today? It's a position we would never choose. Our struggles are real, but God's strength to overcome obstacles matches them. He is friend to the friendless, father to orphans, and husband to widows, providing an abundance of comfort, love, and compassion. Can families survive the travel lifestyle without God? I know I could not. He calls to me, "Be courageous. I am here with you. Do not be afraid." Then He gets into the boat with me and the wind dies down.

CHAPTER TWO

Peggy Sue's Story

He tends his flock like a shepherd: He gathers the lambs in his arms
and carries them close to his heart; he gently leads
those that have young.

—*ISAIAH 40:11*

L OOK, MAMA! ALL THE CARS ARE PULLING OVER. We have the whole
road to ourselves," ten-year-old AmyRose called from the back
of the van.

With all my strength I tugged on the steering wheel, trying to silence the stuck horn. For weeks the horn seemed controlled by a mind
of its own, honking whenever it would be most embarrassing.

Sitting next to me up front, Leilani, age eight, leaned her head back
against the seat and groaned, "We've cleared downtown again."

"Look at the bright side," I hollered over the blaring horn. "At least
this time the horn isn't stuck while we drive past a bunch of police
cars."

"How come the horn never gets stuck when Daddy's home?" six-
year-old Holly yelled above the noise.

"Daddy will fix it with his tools," three-year-old Josiah put in.

I sighed. "When he gets home, son, when he gets home."

My husband has a single fault. He is not independently wealthy.
So because our family of seven likes to eat, he has to work, and his
work demands he travel, hence the rub, hence this book. We deeply
enjoy each other's company, and we are a close family. But the pressures and responsibilities of day-to-day living put tremendous de-

mands on a family. My husband's travel schedule depletes our already limited time together and presents unlimited opportunities for character development. Personally, I think it would be easier to be a shallow person!

You see, things don't always run smoothly when Keith is out of town. And since he is my best friend, as well as the big muscles and calm logic in our marriage, I feel like a twin-engine plane piloting on a single engine when he is away. To magnify my off-kilter course, mechanical things go haywire from the moment Keith's plane lifts off. The dishwasher washes without using the soap, the clothes dryer requires three cycles to dry a single load, the cordless telephone will only work if I stand in one place, the dog (*his* dog) chews up my roses, the water pipes burst (twice), the tire goes flat, the refrigerator develops an annoying high pitch whine (so do I), the car horn gets stuck, and the mousetraps get full.

The months when Keith is gone three weeks out of four, I have been known to grumble.

We were expecting our second baby when Keith began traveling. Keith would see new places, the nicest hotels and convention centers, mix with people who seemed to always look their best. I would stay home with our toddler, the family dog, the weeds, the peanut butter jar, and my ever-expanding girth. I felt left behind.

SOME EASIER, SOME TOUGHER

Though we never like to be apart, some of Keith's trips are easier than others. Those tend to be the shorter trips that occur when everyone is emotionally positive. He jets off for a couple of days, and the children and I spend the time together doing usual routines. Other trips are harder on our family. Especially the trips that have coincided with the first half of a pregnancy when I am bedridden with back-to-back migraines and intense nausea.

"Hi, babe. How are you?"

"Oh, Keith. It's been the worst day of my life. This migraine has gone on for four days. It reached a peak this afternoon. Incredible pain. It got so out of control I couldn't stop vomiting."

"Did you call the doctor?"

"Yeah, he prescribed something. But I couldn't get to the pharmacy to pick it up. I called Kathy, and she brought the prescription over. But it didn't work. The pain got worse, and I thought I would die."

"I'm so sorry, babe. How are the children?"

"They've been such a help. I couldn't make it without them. They bring cool cloths for my head, some tea and toast. They sit with me. When they made breakfast, the milk spilled all over the inside of the refrigerator and onto the kitchen floor. I haven't been downstairs yet to see, but they said they cleaned it up. They heated ravioli for dinner, but the dish full of marinara sauce dropped on the [beige] dining room carpet and splashed on the drapes and across the [fabric] dining room chairs. They were pretty upset. I hurt so bad I didn't care about the mess. I told them it was all right, to clean up as best they could, and I would take care of the rest as soon as I can get up. But when they went to the garage for the bottle of carpet spotter, the bottle of floor wax got bumped. It fell and broke on the garage floor. AmyRose says the garage 'got instantly waxed.' "

Keith sighed. "I wish I were there to take care of you. It's been hard to keep my spirits up this trip. This shouldn't have been my trip to take—it's all office politics. It's especially irritating since the office knows how sick you are and how much I am needed at home right now. I'm sorry, babe."

"I know. I love you. Hurry home. I need you."

How Keith Helps Us

- Keith calls when he arrives at each destination. It's good to know how his day is progressing, to discuss what is going on at home, and to make daily decisions together. The children each talk with their dad, asking what it looks like in another state, curious about the time and weather difference, and filling him in on their news. Regular communication keeps us close emotionally though we are apart physically.

- Keith gives me his itinerary of flights, arrival times, hotels, and phone numbers. I find security in knowing where he is and how to reach him.
- Whenever possible, Keith schedules business trips around our family calendar. He will frequently fly all night to be home for the children's piano recitals, science fairs, or orchestra performances. He tries to be home the nights I teach childbirth classes in our home. I have learned for my own safety not to schedule classes when my husband is away.
- He continually counsels me to schedule fewer activities than usual when he is away because I automatically have more work to do in his absence. Too much pressure makes Mama and children tense.
- Keith tries to use the hotel exercise room, watch what he eats, and get some sleep on the plane coming home so he can plug into the family when he arrives. Chances are I'm a bit weary from consecutive twenty-four-hour duty and looking forward to his help.

This year we had chicken pox. A lot of it. For weeks. I was home. A lot. For weeks. One Sunday when Keith was home he suggested I go to church and he stay home with the "spotted" children. "Oh, could I?" I breathed.

Sometimes I need a good solid nap. Sometimes I need to go to bed early. Sometimes I need Keith to get up in the night with the children. (Notice how much of what I need revolves around sleep!)

- Keith has established a family tradition we hold dear. Every Saturday when he is home he cooks breakfast. Keith enjoys cooking, and we enjoy his talents.
- He reassures me that the children and I come before his job. Keith has been away on my birthday but arranged to have a beautiful bouquet of roses delivered. He cooked a special birthday dinner when he came home.
- Our children enjoy simple remembrances from Daddy's trips. Their favorite is postcards from the places Keith has been. Keith brings a postcard home for each child, a special message written on the back. Over the years each child has a collection of post-

cards, but the messages from their father are a lifetime treasure. An added benefit is the fact that postcards are easy to find, as Keith almost never has time for shopping. The children have fun with the shower caps and miniature soaps from the hotels, or tote bags, pens, hats, and other promotional giveaways from the trade shows.

- No matter how late he gets in, the children know their daddy will come kiss them good-night.

- I have encouraged him to visit any sights he can squeeze in on a trip so we know if it is worthwhile visiting as a family later on. A few of Keith's trips have been within driving distance, so the family could drive there together. Keith works while the children and I see the sights. We have evenings together, plus all the driving time. That's my idea of a field trip!

- Keith asks what I need taken care of before he leaves. The moments he carves out to be sure our window wipers are fit for winter weather, the chicken coop is cleaned, and the bills are current demonstrate his love and provision for the children and me. He acknowledges that business trips do not excuse him from his position as head of our family and home. Jetting off into the sunset does not free either of us from our responsibilities to each other or to our children.

Our home was built directly atop a colony of mice and ants. Additionally, our home backs up to open hills, which translates into more mice. For the most part, we coexist amicably—they live outside and we live inside. But the determined little creatures made a run on our pantry just before Keith's first extended trip away. We had cleaned thoroughly and taken the territory back. Keith set a mousetrap as insurance before he left.

Naturally the trap went off the first day Keith was gone. It was midnight before I tackled the job. I put on gloves that went up to my armpits because I couldn't find a sterile body suit. My first choice was to sweep the entire thing into the trash—traps are cheap. But then a second mouse might slip through to our clean pantry before morning. I needed to reset the trap.

There are no directions on those traps that tell you how to set them. Gingerly I tried to set it. Again and again and again. A half hour later it seemed stable. Using the broom handle, I slid the trap back behind the refrigerator, where it remained until Keith returned the next week. Each day I checked the trap, feeling a new wave of independence at facing and conquering this personal challenge. I was so proud. I was woman. I told Keith over the phone. I told my friends. It was my first time on my own, and I could do it. Keith came home and went to the kitchen to admire my handiwork.

"That's really good, babe," he began. "But I could stand on it and it wouldn't go off." I had set it wrong. During the next territory conflict, the mice tried to take the garage. Keith was thoughtful to set six traps—one for each day he was out of town—so I wouldn't need to concern myself with them.

HOW WE HELP KEITH

Contrary to the glamour associated with travel, Keith is alone for the most part in a strange city. He is tired, and time changes seem to always leave him shortchanged on sleep. His schedule is rigorous, taking him to as many as four states plus an appointment in Canada in just four days. Airports are loud and stressful places—everyone is under time pressures. Keith must squeeze his six-foot, three-inch frame (without his cowboy boots) for long hours into airplanes designed to accommodate the average five-foot, nine-inch person. It's easy enough to find the car rental at the airport, but from there he rarely knows which restaurant is worthwhile or if the neighborhood is safe to walk after the sun goes down. He battles weight gain because nearly every activity centers around sitting and eating. Airplanes and convention centers serve mystery meat—some nameless cut stuffed with something green and covered with sauce. Eating is quickly followed by indigestion. Trade shows require long hours on his feet. He's on the job twenty-four hours a day. He doesn't drink, so hanging out in the hotel lounge is not inviting, and once he closes the door to his hotel room, he is far away from all he knows and holds dear, and he is alone.

When Keith returns, there are often small jobs awaiting him, like the mouse I barricaded in the utility closet. Not only is maintenance around our home needed, but his desk at work is piled high. The traveling makes us feel like we are always trying to catch up.

- Following his itinerary allows us to pray for Keith around the clock. Waking in the night with the baby allows me to pray for him at that time.

- Keeping Keith's overnight case packed is a time-saver. We picked up an extra toothpaste and toothbrush, comb, travel-size blow dryer, and small Bible that stay in the case. When it's time to pack, he gathers the appropriate clothes and tosses in the overnight case. The children and I like to tuck in cheery notes, a good book, a sketch pad and pencils, or similar surprises. Reading a book, drawing, or writing has helped Keith take some mental breaks while on the plane or awaiting sleep in his hotel.

- "Do not spend what little time you have together arguing about the time you don't have with him," Mary Ann Froehlich advises in her book *What's a Smart Woman Like You Doing in a Place Like This?* Business trips devour family weekends and evenings, and Keith's long commutes make our time too limited. (My daily commute takes me from upstairs to downstairs.)

The best gift I can give Keith when he returns is a peaceful home and family. He has been on the go and wants most to be home for an evening just with us. Most flights seem to bring him home in the late night hours, so we plan the next evening after work to be special.

- The children like to hang "welcome home" signs, and Josiah takes special delight in cutting up confetti to pour on Keith in celebration of his return.

- I make sure Keith's coffeepot has been deep-cleaned, the bathroom sparkles, the bed sheets are fresh, and a good home-cooked meal is planned because I figure I can offer everything and more than a fine hotel has provided him. (Yes, I do these things when he is home, too.)

HOW I HELP MYSELF

Despite my previous feelings of being left behind, all in all I feel I have the better deal. I've learned to find the humor in difficult situations and be grateful for my abundant blessings.

- I know I miss Keith intensely because we love each other very much.
- I appreciate that my husband has a job that adequately supports our growing family.
- I am doing the job I love most. Of all the opportunities that exist, I want to be a full-time wife, mother, and homemaker above all else.
- My opportunities to experience fulfillment, exercise creativity, and have fun are unlimited. Not everyone gets to do what they love the most with the people they love best.
- The children and I are cozy in our home, surrounded by all that is familiar to us. We are in our own community, close to our usual stops—the church, music lessons, the grocery store, the library, the park. Though Keith is away, my bed is still full of various and sundry little people who seem to find simple comfort in cuddling in Mama and Daddy's bed. I'm lonely for Keith, but I'm not alone.

HOW WE HELP OUR CHILDREN

The traveling has had its effect on our six children as well. Five-year-old Holly asks each morning, "Is Daddy going on a field trip today?" When Estee was six months old, Keith had been gone more than he had been home. For a couple of those precious, early months, Estee would not accept Keith's comfort when she was tired or fussy. She wanted Mama or one of her older sisters to rock her to sleep. Keith was wise enough to rebuild his relationship with his baby daughter.

He laughed and played with Estee, held her frequently, fed her, and changed her diapers. Soon her daddy's voice and arms once again represented comfort and security.

- Our children feel secure when they know the schedule, so we let them know about Keith's upcoming trips as soon as we know.
- We help them find Daddy's destinations on the map, determine how long his flight will take, and count how many days will pass before he returns.
- Keith takes time to explain what he will be doing while he is away, whether he is attending a seminar, meeting with clients, or working a trade show. Even when he is home, Keith helps the children understand his work. At three years of age, Josiah thought Keith's work was merely driving off each morning in his pickup truck and returning again at dinnertime. Josiah told others his dad worked in a truck. The children and I met Keith for lunch one day, and he gave them a tour of his office and the foundry. On short days, one of the children accompanies Keith to work. They see firsthand what their dad does and who he works with. They get a flavor for his days and take a good book along to cover any boring moments.
- We set a high priority on having dinner as a family, enjoying regular family devotions each evening, and attending church together.
- When he's home, Keith and I set an evening aside each week to talk. On those nights, the children have their dinner before Keith comes home. Then we spend some time with the children taking a walk, playing a game, or whatever else they want to do. After devotions, the children are tucked into bed, the older ones with a good book, while Keith and I have a late dinner by the fireplace. Keeping our family's stress level at a minimum is something we must guard continuously.

HOW FRIENDS HELP

When Keith is gone, I do not accept invitations that do not include our children. Yet our social life cannot be put on hold each time Keith leaves. The children and I attend church activities, keep up with music lessons, go on field trips, visit friends, and accept invitations whenever feasible. Mary Ann sent an invitation to her son's first birthday party. "Could the children and I come even though Keith is out of town?" I asked.

"Of course," she laughed. "If I didn't do anything without John, I wouldn't do much."

For a long time, I did not do special things without Keith because I didn't want to leave him out. He finally convinced me that he didn't feel left out. He wanted the children and me to enjoy every opportunity as his gift to us.

THE STRUGGLE CONTINUES

For Keith it is a Catch-22 situation. The job is his vehicle to care for his family, but the job is also what takes him away from his family. After one flurry of travel, Keith was home and our family settled in for our evening devotions. It was three-year-old Josiah's turn to pray.

"Dear Lord, help Daddy be home for dinner . . ."

My eyes met Keith's.

" . . . thank you for helping us do what is right, and help Daddy come home for dinner . . ."

I held up my finger for a count of two.

" . . . and help us to be able to go to Marine World to see the whales and dolphins, and help Daddy come home for dinner . . ."

I added a third finger to the count.

" . . . and help us to sleep good, and help Daddy be home for dinner . . ."

I raised a fourth finger and my eyebrows for emphasis.

" . . . and help Ruby [the dog] not to chew up Mama's roses, and help Daddy be home for dinner . . ."

When the prayer was done, Keith whispered, "I got the message!"

When the travel has been intense, Keith finds creative ways to let me know he is leaving again. There is the phone call from work:

"Hi, babe," he says in *that* tone of voice.

"When do you have to leave?" I accuse in *that* tone of voice.

My favorite approach is when we are talking with friends after church and Keith happens to let it drop that he will be out of town during such and such a week. My eyebrows go up in surprise. "News to me," I quip, aware that this is not the place for an emotional reaction.

"Just haven't had a chance to tell you yet," Keith replies.

When Keith is out of town, I do my best to care for our children and the home. I keep up family devotions with the children, and Keith maintains his own Bible reading and prayer time. Without a doubt, our faith in God and our relationship with Him and with one another keeps our family strong and focused.

This past decade of business travel has given me a taste of single parenting, and it's an overwhelming job. I am ever more grateful for my life's partner and the simple ways we support each other. I have learned that short-circuiting van horns is a temporary condition, and a reminder of the value of a good sense of humor. Gathering me in His arms, I am confident God shepherds our family. I know He carries us close to His heart and gently leads me.

CHAPTER THREE

The Men's Side

The righteous man leads a blameless life;
blessed are his children after him.

—*PROVERBS 20:7*

FREQUENT TRAVELING AND AN OVERLOADED SCHEDULE had made Keith difficult to reach by phone. One customer left numerous messages on Keith's voice mail until one day the customer called again and Keith picked up the phone. "This is Keith," he answered.

"Is this God?" came the reply.

"No, just Keith," my husband smiled.

"Right," the customer agreed. "God is easier to get ahold of!"

JOHN'S STORY

Enough of the serious side! As I tell my wife, I "don't do deep." Of course I would not choose to travel. I love my family—I totally enjoy being a dad and spending time with my children. But I do need to make a living to support them, and this job is what I know how to do. Besides family issues, there are other reasons I do not care to travel. And what has convinced me this lifestyle is less than glamorous? How about the time . . .

- I discovered my reserved hotel room was in a questionable part of town (the armed guards and the bars on the windows were my first clue). I barely slept as pieces of the ceiling fell on me all night.

- A fellow traveler picked up my suitcase at the airport and I took his identical bag. I ended up in my room with size 46 suits and I'm sure he wondered where the "Thumbelina" suits in his bag came from.

- Arriving late in a small town, I asked the car rental clerk where I could board the shuttle to find my rental car, and he replied, "What's a shuttle?"

- In one hotel room I heard explosions and thought it was an unusual time of year for thunderstorms. Then the evening news reported a bank bombing by terrorists, showing my hotel building . . . *my room* . . . above the twisted wreckage.

- My heavy suitcase fell out of the overhead rack on the plane and almost knocked me unconscious. The flight attendant had assured me that the bag was secure, and she begged me not to sue the airlines.

- A passenger assigned next to me came running aboard the plane carrying a large pizza. She put it under her seat as carry-on luggage, and the pizza slid onto my briefcase during takeoff. I said, "Excuse me, madam, your pizza is on my briefcase." She picked it up and proceeded to eat it (halfway in my lap). She didn't even offer me a piece! All my presentations during that trip smelled like pepperoni pizza.

- I've awakened in a hotel room and can't remember what city I am in until I check the phone book in the nightstand.

Is traveling an experience to be envied? No . . . it is a sacrifice I make to support the people I love most.

Keith's Story

Travel sounds glamorous to those who don't. I guess the first couple of trips were exciting. The rest have gone a lot like this:

The flight with my boss from Oakland, California, to Chicago's O'Hare International Airport should have lasted three hours and forty-five minutes. The trip proceeded according to schedule until just outside Chicago when the pilot announced our plane would be put into a holding pattern for at least thirty minutes due to a major thunderstorm directly over O'Hare. Our plane, along with fifty other large aircraft, began circling the airport like a swarm of bees. Looking out the window, I felt like I was part of a hanging crib mobile. At one point, our pilot cut back the engine because another airplane was too close above us. My body was suddenly airborne, like when you go over a hill in the car fast.

The control tower requested we circle another forty-five minutes, but lacking fuel, we diverted to Des Moines, Iowa. Twenty-five other planes came with us. The airport was jammed with unexpected planes landing all at once. We sat on the Des Moines runway for ninety minutes because no gates could accommodate us. I didn't want to go to Des Moines anyway.

By this time I had finished my book and all the work I had brought along. I tried to call my wife from the plane, but the satellite was jammed with other passengers' calls.

We finally disembarked for a short refuel and rest-room break at the gate farthest from all gift shops, restaurants, and other forms of civilization. Smokers puffed as many cigarettes as they could in the forty-five minutes. I got back on the plane to breathe.

We flew back to Chicago. Because of the backup, it took another forty-five minutes to get the boss's suitcase. I learned long ago to take my luggage on the plane with me as carry-on.

Now all the rental car counters were closed at the airport, and the shuttle circles the area only every thirty minutes. We came out of the terminal just as the shuttle pulled away. At least the storm was over.

Halfway through the paper work process at the car rental agency, a second storm cut the power off. All computers were out. The clerk had to finish the paper work manually by flashlight. "Take my advice," he offered as he handed us the keys, "get out of here and don't ever come back."

Our hotel was another hour away. We could have flown into Milwaukee, which would have been fifteen minutes from our appointment, but the guy who booked the trip . . .

Just outside Racine, Wisconsin, we found the only fast-food place open and grabbed a hamburger. We had it "our way" all night long. I climbed into bed at 2:00 A.M. after requesting a 6:00 A.M. wake-up call. All night I heard the constant sound of water dripping: Was it the hotel's cooling system or just a fitting end to my day?

Fueled only by caffeine, the next day we met with the largest construction equipment manufacturer in the world to give them a piece of our minds, which we had left somewhere between Des Moines and Chicago.

Back home, PeggySue had one child with a 104° temperature, and two others who needed to play in the community youth orchestra some forty minutes away. Over the phone I could hear the tears in my wife's voice as she struggled with not being able to be both at the concert for the older girls and at home with our sick son. I was all too familiar with not being able to be in two places at the same time. Neither of us felt good about the children performing without either parent in the audience. It just didn't seem right.

Flying home the next day, I put my thoughts on paper in the form of a letter to my wife.

Dear Love,

As I'm flying back home to you, I'm thinking about the kind of weekend you've had with me gone on business and the kids not feeling well.

I feel a sense of bitterness from you toward my travel and toward myself as well. Traveling is hardest on the family—there is no doubt in my mind. Travel is also hard on the traveler, not because of airplanes, hotels, and working long hours, but because I can't help with situations that arise like I could if I were home. It's a very helpless, hopeless feeling that can make me resent my job, career, and financial situation. I start to question my ability to be a good husband and father. If I were a good husband, I would always be there to help when times get tough, when times get frustrating. I would be there when we should be celebrating together over some great news. If I were a good father, I would never miss an event my children participated in. I would be available to comfort those hurts that always seem to happen while I'm gone.

But for all the feelings I go through, you have many more, and you have many more responsibilities when I'm gone. I want you to know I understand your frustrations and resentments toward the traveling. I'm confused about how to fix these things. In theory, my job and career, my family and goals, should be controlled and directed by me. But that isn't the way it seems to work.

Day to day, week to week, month to month, it all runs together, and before long, time has slipped by and I feel guilty for not doing more for you and more for the kids. You and the children are flying in multiple directions with school, music, field trips, etc. I'm glad you're having fun, but I'm also envious. I'm having a hard time lately trying to remember what "fun" is. I move from crisis to crisis, bandaging this problem or that problem, taking on more and more burdens, and having less and less time to actually sit back and think about what we should be wanting out of life.

My priorities are a great marriage, a happy family, loving children, a job that supports us, a comfortable home, time to have fun as a family and individually, and health for all of us.

We can't achieve any of this if we don't have God as our foundation and walk our lives according to His ways. We also cannot have the above if we are over-burdened with work, worry, guilt, frustration, bitterness, and resentment. Each of these areas requires time and effort. Of those two items, time seems to be the premium commodity we are running short on.

My commute time in hours robs us of an additional twenty-five days per year over and above the time I'm away on business trips. This is something we must discuss. We have to consider what amount of commute time is acceptable for our lives—whether we should move closer to the job or change jobs.

For you, the largest time robber, I would think, is the cleaning and maintenance of the house. Perhaps we should look into getting you some help. Establishing low maintenance landscape with automatic sprinklers will free up some of the time spent on yard work.

I want to fix this fast-moving train. You and I together need to stop and think through just exactly what we are going to do with our family and our current pace of life.

Babe, I am committed to you and our children for life. You never need to doubt my love for you. I will do whatever we prayerfully decide as a couple to do with our lives. Now is the time to stop the frustration and bitterness toward circumstances and take control of our lives as far as is possible. Let's talk and talk some more. I love you so much!

Keith

CHAPTER FOUR

Raising Babies and Young Children With a Traveling Father

The Lord answered, "Who then is the faithful and wise manager, whom the master puts in charge of his servants to give them their food allowance at the proper time? It will be good for that servant whom the master finds doing so when he returns. I tell you the truth, he will put him in charge of all his possessions.

—LUKE 12:42–44

D ISCOURAGED AND EXHAUSTED *with the sheer volume of work involved in parenting a household of small children, my days were a blur of changing diapers, tackling the never-ending laundry pile (Mt. Never-rest), struggling to keep the home reasonably neat, and getting regular meals on the table. Every day the same things needed to be done.*

One evening as I was reading Luke 12:42–44, I realized the Lord had given me these children to care for, and should the Lord return today and find me changing diapers, doing laundry, and cooking meals for my family, He would find me being that faithful and wise steward. Knowing I am doing what my Lord has set before me, His servant, has elevated the daily tasks above drudgery to important service to my family and the Lord.

—Kathleen Quinn

———

Raising babies and young children is a challenging time of life. It requires teamwork from both parents. Sleepless nights and exhaustion are part of the job description. What happens when part of the team is missing?

A Young Mother's Story
by Debbie Karlik

I remember that morning four and a half years ago when I called the doctor's office to find out the results of a test. "Congratulations!" said the cheery nurse. "You're going to have a baby." I wanted to say, "Thanks, but I already have a baby." Joey was seven months old; I didn't feel the need for another baby, especially since this would be my fourth child.

I desperately wanted to talk to my husband, but he was out of town and couldn't be reached. So I dialed dear old Mom and Dad, my greatest support system, 2,000 miles away. After hearing my disheartened hello, Mom asked, "What's wrong?"

"Oh, Mom," I cried, and she immediately knew the answer. That baby, thereafter known as my "Oh, Mom Baby," ushered in the beginning of the toughest part of my life.

My husband and greatest friend, Bill, works for an oil company. He started minimal traveling about eight years ago, or two kids ago. It was kind of fun for me. It made his job seem important and glamorous. I was eager to see him pull into the driveway, or better yet, to go to the airport to greet him. I was excited to see if he brought me anything.

Gradually the travel increased. We were transferred a few times, but our young children were relatively unaffected by the changes. In fact, we often traveled with Bill. I was homeschooling the children, so we could always be together as a family. It was a fun and exciting time for all of us.

But as Bill's job description changed, the travel increased, and we had two more babies. By the time our fourth child was due, Bill's job required him to be gone nearly every week. My life was in constant upheaval. Bill was often required to move to the new location immediately, while I remained behind to tie up loose ends such as selling the house. With a seven-year-old, a five-year-old, a sixteen-month-old, and a one-week-old baby, you can imagine the stress of keeping the house presentable for viewing.

After selling our home, we had to move into an apartment for a few weeks. Our neighbors complained that they could hear everything that happened in our apartment, day and night. They knew when I got up to nurse the baby, when we took showers—*everything*—and they told us about it.

Bill's travel schedule became most difficult for me after our last move. Knowing I had to maintain the home front alone made it hard to get out of bed each morning. I sometimes found myself wishing that I didn't have so many children. What kind of mother would wish such a terrible thing? I had always loved being a mom, but I didn't like doing the job by myself.

Many times a day my children would ask, "When will Daddy come home?" It made me sad to look into their big, brown eyes and say, "Not today." I grew even sadder when they stopped asking.

I recently asked my oldest son how he felt when his dad missed a game or special school event. He said, "I would have done better if Daddy had been there." Inside, I said, "Me too."

One morning while Bill was traveling, I needed to be up and in the shower by 6:30 A.M. so I could get the children to school, where I would work in the classroom. I planned to take my other two children to my neighbor's house. I woke up at 7:30 . . . need I say more? I sped through the morning routine. My oldest son insisted every article of clothing he owned was in the dirty clothes pile and that I hadn't done any laundry since last Thanksgiving. My daughter's class was dressing in tropical clothing for "Tropical Day" but I hadn't heard about it until now. My second son was crying because he wanted to go to school with me. The baby was still asleep. I had to take him in his pajamas (without breakfast) to my neighbor's, and he was not a happy camper.

After making lunches, fixing hair, packing bags, and remembering the bananas for "Tropical Day," I piled everyone into the car and headed for my neighbor's house. As we backed out of the garage, my daughter said she had forgotten her sunglasses for Tropical Day. We didn't have time to go back into the house.

That's when I remembered the traffic ticket Bill received for running a stop sign. He hadn't paid it and his court date was in five minutes. As we pulled up at the school, my daughter mumbled something about being the only one in her class without sunglasses. Naturally, I dropped everyone off and dashed home to get them. I think when fathers travel, mothers tend to compensate in other areas. My daughter may not have a father in town, but she was sure going to have sunglasses! I could control that.

I realize that these hard days are part of motherhood and all mothers face them. But I wanted Bill to be there, to come alongside to help me. I desired his companionship more than anything. But my deep-rooted faith clung tightly to God's promises, knowing God would help me handle this.

My parents and my friends in town have been my support system. Just having someone recognize that my life is difficult has been a great help. My church family has also actively shown their love and support. And God has sustained our family through the stressful times.

At one point, when my life became tougher, I told Bill, "I can handle this, and I will handle it with God's grace, but I don't think it's good for me. I don't like the mother I am becoming."

Within the week came another job change. This one involved much less travel but a long commute and extended hours. Bill was not home any more than before, and he wasn't happy in the job.

After much heartache and prayer, he took a new position across the country with shorter hours, no commute, and no travel. Bill moved immediately, while I have remained here to sell our house and allow the older children to finish the school year. Upheaval and survival are the norm again. I will have to leave my local support system, but God is good. Soon our family will all be together again.

RAISING BABIES . . . AND TEENS?
DEBBIE HABEGGER'S STORY

Debbie appeared to have the perfect life . . . a loving husband, a committed faith, a beautiful home, and two successful teenagers. Yet unexpectedly her entire life changed. Debbie and her husband, Dean, became the proud parents of twins!

Debbie and Dean were not new to the travel lifestyle. As a sales manager, Dean had traveled for over a decade. Each year, as his responsibilities increased, his travel increased too. Travel creates a challenge for raising any family, but how does one raise "two families"—two babies and two teens? Debbie's story follows:

It is a typical day in our household. Dean is out of town, and I live in a perpetual state of exhaustion. I wake the twins at 4:30 A.M. to make the one-hour drive to the airport. I often make this drive when one of our cars is unavailable. (Our twins have learned to sleep well in the car.) I am up until midnight the night before helping our teenagers with their homework. I also have a full day of laundry ahead of me and other preparations for our son Ryan's weekend church trip.

My toddler twins are running everywhere. They especially like to climb on counters or sit in the kitchen sink and turn the water on. I discover that our daughter Kylie left a tube of lipstick in her jeans pocket and it is all over Ryan's best clothes. A good part of the afternoon will be spent trying to salvage them with a toothbrush and cleaning solutions. The twins are happily (too quietly) sitting in the kitchen, pulling a bug apart . . . and eating it.

Am I having a bad day? No, this is a normal day, requiring me to be in too many places at the same time. But I love my family. Deeply committed to living my life with no regrets, I try to make the most of every moment.

I have not slept well in two years. The twins wake up at night to be fed (of course, never at the same time). I have run on sheer adrenaline and God's grace. Dean partners with me in parenting our children. He gets up at night to help with the twins. He helps drive our teens to their numerous activities. Ironically, it is his support that makes Dean's weekly absence so difficult when he is traveling. I need him. I need another pair of hands. This is a job I cannot do alone.

When the twins arrived, Dean and I made it a conscious choice *not* to change our teenagers' lives. Friends would remark, "At least you have built-in baby-sitters." We don't look at it that way. We have busy teens who need to be parented and supported as they always have been. We are committed to being at all their activities to cheer them on, no matter how inconvenient it may be. We regularly attend sports events, band reviews, church functions, cheerleading activities, and more. We don't add extra chores to their lives.

Dean and I constantly balance the carpool schedule, deciding which one of us will attend which event. The twins go everywhere with us, running at full speed . . . in opposite directions.

But when Dean is traveling, the burden rests entirely on my shoulders. It helps that I love being a mother and being with my children. I love staying up at night talking with them about their concerns. I love having their friends over. I enjoy participating on school committees. I am happy to have active teens who channel their time in healthy ways. We celebrate everything; even the day's football game calls for a football candle in Ryan's breakfast.

Dean makes sacrifices too. He arranges his travel schedule to be there for our teens. He has flown home early for many a concert or game. Not wanting to uproot our family, Dean has turned down job positions that would require relocation. We try to appreciate the sacrifices that each of us are making.

Our children tell me that they do not feel their father's weekly absence is a serious loss because their own lives are so busy and Dean stays in daily contact with them. They miss him, but they feel loved and important to him. They understand the limitations of his job.

Our children remain our top priority, and they know we respect them. Driving my children to their activities has become our special "alone time" to talk and pray. At breakfast we read from our favorite devotional book and stay connected during the day through prayer. The Lord is the foundation for survival in our home.

Some days I wonder how I can be all things to all people. Well-meaning friends advise, "Watch out! You can't do it all. You need to take care of yourself." I try to stay focused on the larger picture. When my seventeen-year-old son runs to give me a big hug in front of the whole football team and says, "I love you, Mom. I'm so glad you're here at the game," then I know that I am doing the right thing. Next year my son will leave for college, and these opportunities will be gone. I don't want to miss one of them. I dread the first time that Dean is traveling and Ryan is gone.

In essence, we are raising two families in the face of a challenging travel career. Yes, I am exhausted. But I cling to a higher purpose that cannot be erased by the stress of travel. It is beautifully said in a verse handed down in our family: "I have no greater joy than to hear that my children are walking in the truth" (3 John 4).

AWAY FOR HALF THE YEAR
BY JIM GOLDEN

I work with a lot of fellows who have gone through several marriages and families because they refused to put their family first and work on their problems. They view travel as a way to escape. Since I spend half the year away from my family, this is an attractive option—leave the problems behind. But I know too many co-workers who have returned home to find their wives and children gone, their houses and bank accounts empty.

I don't know if I have found the balance yet. When I am overseas, I try to show my interest and concern for my family through e-mail and phone calls. I spend much time praying for my family. I ask God to guide me as a parent, showing me what is right and what needs improvement on my next visit home.

Then when I come home, I don't work at all. I focus entirely on my family and our church. My greatest struggle is trying to decide the right time to leave this job to find a more normal assignment.

"MY DADDY LIVES IN ANGOLA"
DEBBIE GOLDEN'S STORY

A financial analyst with a major oil company, my husband, Jim, works six months a year in Angola. The ongoing rotation of one month overseas and one month at home has radically changed our lives for the past three years. I feel I have two separate lives, one with Jim and one without him.

Jim helicopters into a camp in Angola, which he is unable to leave until he returns home. The camp has come under fire similar to guerrilla warfare tactics, and although the camp is secure, I still fear for his safety.

I also fear for my safety. We have two young boys. The first thing we did when Jim accepted this position was to install an alarm system so that I could sleep at night. The boys and I rarely go out after dark. We especially miss Jim on holidays and weekends when the rest of the world is enjoying "family time."

Like most other wives of traveling husbands, initially I thought I could do it all. I would simply take over Jim's responsibilities as well as mine. One Saturday morning, leaving our two young boys watching television, I went outside to mow the grass. I came in a few minutes later to find the baby had poured cereal all over himself and the room was in chaos. I knew then that I needed some help.

Others in our situation had hired gardeners, nannies, and various types of household help, which I had thought extravagant. I now see that help is necessary to survival. A wife especially appreciates a husband hiring those services before he leaves for the field.

Jim prepares us well for his trips, but he could not prepare us for everything. As a baby, our second son, John, was constantly sick. I spent endless hours in the doctor's office. I needed another pair of hands night and day. John's speech is delayed, and we wonder if it's a result of his numerous illnesses and ear infections or an emotional response to Jim's absences. And was his constant illness part of a cycle of stress for both mother and child?

I always dread Jim's departure. I used to experience a panic response, the fright/flight reaction. I would begin withdrawing emotionally from our relationship to survive the coming pain and separation. We both knew this was unhealthy and had to work through the issue.

The children and I know that we are a priority in Jim's life. Jim often writes or e-mails us. He draws pictures of the animals he sees in Angola for the boys. This is a language they can understand.

We always celebrate Daddy's arrival home. One week ahead, we begin a countdown. Then we meet him at the airport, go out to dinner, and the vacation begins!

I have many close, supportive friends who help me in Jim's absence, but the problem is that Jim is my *best* friend. When Jim comes home, I breathe a great sigh of relief. My partner is home to share the load.

Our children are much happier when Jim is home. Their individual temperaments govern their responses to his return. Our older son, Lee, is our "microwave" child. He immediately becomes Dad's buddy and all is right with the world. Our second son, John, is a "slow cooker" with a more reserved personality. It takes him time to warm up to Dad.

The greatest changes in my life have been spiritual. Like many other adults, I had baggage from my past that I had never dealt with. Jim's absence forced me to tackle those issues on my own, searching the Scriptures, attending Bible studies, and developing a deeper relationship with God. I have learned that it is okay to need other people. Jim cannot meet all my needs. He once told me, "Isolation breeds contempt." He knew that my isolation during his absence would only cause further problems. He encouraged me to develop relationships. This personal growth has been the most positive result of Jim's travels. It has enriched our marriage and my other family relationships as well. We are called to work out our salvation with fear and trembling (Philippians 2:12), and that is what I've been doing these past few years. We are not called to be comfortable but to grow.

EPILOGUE

When Jim and Debbie were expecting their third child, Jim was transferred to Papua New Guinea. Since technology was not available in the new location to accommodate Debbie's condition, Debbie and their sons lived with Debbie's mother in the southern United States, while Jim worked overseas. Toward the end of her pregnancy, Debbie flew to Australia, where Jim met her for the birth of their daughter.

Then the family joined Jim in Papua New Guinea. Later the Goldens moved back to the United States.

STRATEGY

Here are suggestions that have helped these families handle the travel lifestyle.

For Husbands and Wives

- Foremost, live your life without regrets. Enjoy each other and treasure the years when your children are young and at home. These precious years pass all too quickly.
- Make your faith in God the common foundation of your family through regular Bible reading, prayer, and involvement with your church.

For the Traveler

- Parenting when the children are small is perhaps the most physically demanding. When you are home, give your wife a much-needed break. When her batteries are charged, she will better handle the times when you are away.
- Arrive home with a big hug for your life's partner and words of appreciation and encouragement for her and the children.
- Provide ways for your wife to catch up on much-needed rest, with naps and opportunities to sleep in.
- Help with family responsibilities: change diapers, prepare some meals, get up with the children during the night.
- Play with your children. Read bedtime stories to them. Pray with them, and tuck them into bed.
- Attend to household maintenance. Run the vacuum, do some laundry, oversee the yard work.
- Before you leave on your next business trip, make sure your wife and children are safe and comfortable. Be sure your house is in good repair and the car is in good operating condition.

- Pay the bills.
- Secure backup support for your family through extended family, trusted friends, and the church while you are away.
- Whenever possible, take the family along on trips.
- Even if it means flying all night, schedule trips so you can "be there" for the baseball game, the recital, the play, or the birthday.
- While away, call home daily. Share your day with your wife, and listen to her news. Talk with each of the children. Even if the baby can't talk yet, the familiar sound of your voice over the phone will strengthen your relationship with that child.
- Use the phone to oversee business matters for the family. If the house is for sale, keep in touch with the Realtor and title company by phone. Your five-minute phone call made to take care of pending issues strongly demonstrates your care for your wife as she holds down the fort in your absence.

For the Fort Soldier

- Cling to God for your strength. Spend regular time in Bible reading and prayer, even if it is only five minutes.
- Enjoy your children. With one parent frequently away, perhaps your greatest calling is to be the anchor, totally available to them. Pray with your children, play with them, read to them.
- Greet your daily responsibilities cheerfully. Doing the laundry and changing diapers is noble and honorable work.
- In a blank book, record the cute things your children say. Keep the camera loaded with film to catch those once-in-a-lifetime moments. A video camera may be a worthwhile investment.
- Schedule time to rest. If the children nap, use that time for personal rest, whether that means devotions, reading an inspirational book, pursuing a hobby, or taking your own nap.
- Try to get to bed at a reasonable hour. As the only parent "on call," you may be up in the night with a restless little one. Adequate rest does wonders for your patience and sense of humor.
- Stay involved in your local church. The church will be a dynamic support for you physically, emotionally, and spiritually.

For the Church and Others

- Offer to transport the children to school, church, or other activities. This simple gift may allow the mother to stay home so the baby (or she) can get a nap.
- If you will be running errands, offer to pick up a few groceries, stamps from the post office, or return library books and videos.
- Invite the family for social activities, even when the dad is out of town.
- Attend the children's special events when their dad is not able to. Though you certainly can't take Dad's place, your presence bolsters the celebration.
- Call once in a while just to see how things are going.
- Offer to care for the children should a need arise. Specify days and times that are most convenient for you.
- Tell your friend she can call you in case of an emergency, even in the middle of the night.
- Take the family some soup or a simple meal, especially if there is illness in the home.
- Keep the family in your prayers.
- Speak words of encouragement.

CHAPTER FIVE

Raising Teens With a Traveling Father

Sons are a heritage from the Lord, children a reward from him. Like arrows in the hands of a warrior are sons born in one's youth. Blessed is the man whose quiver is full of them. They will not be put to shame when they contend with their enemies in the gate.

—PSALM 127:3–5

WHEN MY DAD FIRST STARTED TRAVELING, *we drifted apart. We weren't close anymore. It was awkward when he was home for any length of time. He had his schedule and his habits, and we had our new ones. They sometimes conflicted. I learned to ask my mom questions that I would have previously asked my dad. Now my mom is the one I answer to on a daily basis. When dad is home, it seems strange to ask him. On the positive side, my dad and I have grown closer together again. My sister and I have learned to handle more responsibility. My dad's travel has bonded my mom, my sister, and me closer together.*

—Jennifer Taylor, eighteen years old

I hate the fact that my dad goes out of town often. When he started going out of town every week, I had to learn to do things my mom didn't have time for anymore, such as cooking meals for myself. I became more independent. When my dad was in town, our home was filled with tension. He would try to do things for me that I was now used to doing myself. He would offer to help me, I would get annoyed with him asking, and he would be hurt. I was comfortable in my new ways, and he wasn't used to it.

My dad has learned that if I want help, I'll ask for it. The only positive

things I've discovered about his traveling are the frequent flyer miles and
learning to do more things for myself. I would not recommend this situation,
though.

—Brieanne Taylor, fifteen years old

———

Teens need the most secure home foundation possible to negotiate those turbulent years. Loss of a parent due to divorce or death is especially damaging during this critical life stage, so how does the loss of a dad to travel affect teenagers?

RIDING A BICYCLE UPHILL
BY CHRISTI TAYLOR

Our family enjoyed an unusually stable homelife until a few years ago when Ken's job required him to begin traveling Monday through Friday each week. Our lives changed overnight. Previously Ken had been home every night. He read to Jennifer and Brieanne, prayed with them and talked with them nightly. Because he was such a devoted father, his sudden absence left a bigger hole.

Working full-time as a school librarian, I counted on my husband's help in raising our active teens. He transported the girls to and from their many activities. Now I found myself a single parent during the week.

I felt angry, abandoned. I resented Ken's absence. I had married for companionship. Now the rules had changed. But one thing had not changed—we were still committed to keeping our marriage and family together.

The travel lifestyle is like constantly riding a bicycle uphill. If I don't give up, the ride can make me and my family stronger. Forced to think and react creatively, I try to rise to the challenge rather than allow the difficulties to destroy me. My faith in Jesus Christ gives me the resources.

Keeping the situation in perspective helps. Not long after Ken began traveling, one of my closest friends lay dying of cancer, leaving behind her husband and two young sons. As I nursed her during those last days, I would think, "How dare I complain? Our struggles are nothing compared to theirs."

Families face many types of adversity and loss. Travel is *not* the issue. How we face our trial *is* the issue. I determined to bring good out of a difficult situation. Once I worked through my roller coaster emotions, I realized what our teenage girls needed most was consistency. The rules of our home have not changed because Ken is traveling. If the girls ask to do something that I know Ken would not allow, we talk with him on the phone that night before making a decision. If the decision needs to be made immediately, I deliver the bad news.

Being both Mom and Dad all week takes most of my energy. I try to focus the rest on our marriage, but my best intentions can be sabotaged. I tend to be a controlling person, worrying and becoming angry when life does not go according to plan. So when Ken calls home nightly, I try to remember to listen to him and not spend the time complaining about things he cannot do anything about.

To cope with my anger I often write Ken a letter. Depending on how fiery the letter is, I may or may not give it to him. I'm learning to trust God by praying and immersing myself in Scriptures such as "Trust in the Lord with all your heart and lean not on your own understanding; in all your ways acknowledge him, and he will make your paths straight" (Prov. 3:5–6). I ask God to encourage me and heal the hurts and disappointments.

When Ken returns from a trip, we experience a short adjustment period. When the tension builds, we chuckle and say "reentry." When Ken is home, we try to reconnect as a couple when the girls are busy with their own activities. We don't want to infringe on their only time with Dad. We must grab each moment we can as a family.

At a stage in life when other teens are separating from family activities, we're grateful our daughters make it a priority to spend time with us. Though our daughters are constantly on the run, I try to visit their world often. For example, Brieanne and I will meet Jennifer during her break at work. When Ken is in town, he tries to pick the girls up from school, take them out for coffee, and spend personal time with them. Convinced that they will base their decision about a future spouse on their dad's example, he tries to be involved in every aspect of their lives.

With college around the corner for Jennifer, I asked God to show me that her faith is solid. She and I made a trip out of state to visit a potential college. My fear of flying justified itself when shortly after takeoff the pilot announced we were returning to the airport because our landing gear apparently wasn't working. We circled the airport watching fire engines race down the runway. The crew prepared us for a crash-landing. I was terrified. How would Ken and Brieanne survive such a tragedy?

Jennifer saw my fear. "Mom, we are going to be okay," she said. "Even if we die today, we will be okay. We belong to God."

The landing gear did work and we returned to the ground, celebrating God's protection on our lives. And I celebrated God's answer: Jennifer's faith was rock solid.

The traveler's life is completely unpredictable. We must cherish each moment God allows us to spend together. "Who of you by worrying can add a single hour to his life? But seek first his kingdom and his righteousness, and all these things will be given to you as well. Therefore do not worry about tomorrow, for tomorrow will worry about itself. Each day has enough trouble of its own" (Matt. 6:27, 33–34).

ADJUSTING TO THE SEPARATION
BY KEN TAYLOR

What makes travel difficult isn't the distance but the separation from my family. Things they were eager to discuss on Tuesday are forgotten by Saturday. My family has become accustomed to functioning without me, and when I get home they're no longer eager to welcome me back.

I don't think I balance traveling, career, family, and my spiritual walk well. I *know* my spiritual walk is most important, but an observer assessing my life might say my priorities are career/travel, family, and then my spiritual walk. Daily I struggle to keep my relationship with the Lord first, to keep spending time in God's Word. Each day I pray that I will model Christian values in my relationships with subordinates, peers, and superiors.

I've also learned about boundaries and precautions. To protect my marriage, I don't allow opportunities to be alone with a female co-worker. After-hours meetings take place with groups, and I don't inquire about personal matters. I keep my compliments on professional matters, never on personal appearance. As married men who travel, we need to keep our personal lives private and our business relationships just that—business.

IT'S EASIER TO PARENT TEENAGERS
BY LORIE POPE

I enjoyed the stage of life when my children were young, but it was exhausting. My mother encouraged me not to accept comments like "Wait until they are teenagers, then you will have trouble." Those were some of the best years of her parenting.

I took her advice. I expected to enjoy my children's teen years and told them so. Our sons are now ten, thirteen, fifteen, and eighteen, and indeed these are rich and full years. We still have challenges, but we can work through them.

Bob and I married young, and he traveled extensively the first thirteen years of his career, gone almost every week for two to four days. I stayed home with the boys, first doing day care, then teaching piano lessons. I struggled with his being gone until God showed me my husband's travel was in His will. I was at peace with that.

Still I ached for the boys when Dad could not be there for school activities. The older boys, Karl and Trevor, especially enjoy playing basketball, fishing, and hunting with their father. I could fish, but the rest . . . Bob was too tired on the weekends to do much else but rest and tend to minimum household maintenance that absolutely had to be done.

The times of separation became more difficult as our children entered their teens. Our youngest two sons, Jordan and Taylor, didn't know what it was like to have Dad around. We saw the time going by quickly and realized that very soon the oldest boys would go off to college.

Having the evening meal together keeps our family close-knit. With Bob gone so often, I try to make this time special. Occasionally having a pizza night at home, or going out for fast food, not only breaks up the time Bob is gone, but since food is a big priority for my growing sons, it's also a way of making home attractive to their friends.

To maintain our spiritual balance, many years ago we began a tradition of evening family devotions with the boys. We read from a contemporary version of the Bible or read stories from *Guideposts* magazine. We discuss what is happening in the news, relating these issues to our faith. We pray together, talk through disputes, and end the day at peace with one another. Bob leads this devotional time when he is home, and even when he is away, we pray together over the phone.

Our children give mixed reviews of their dad's traveling. I think that is good. I'm glad they miss their dad when he is gone. However, we try to keep life interesting when he is away too. The boys agree that's when some of our most exciting moments occur. We've had our share of bike accidents, broken bones, and overflowing toilets.

God has used negative situations to teach our boys tenderness, compassion, and caring. I have fibromyalgia, a condition similar to rheumatoid arthritis that affects muscles instead of joints. It can be quite painful, draining my energy. The boys have developed a helpful attitude, often carrying groceries, cleaning the house, and doing other challenging tasks—especially when Dad isn't home. They have gained some skills and independence they might not otherwise have acquired.

The day arrived, however, when a job transfer came through and God confirmed it was time to make a change. We chose not to move with the company to a larger city. Everyone in the family agreed to do with less in order to stay near grandparents who could participate in significant family events.

After many months of job searching, Bob found a position that didn't involve extensive travel. We paid a price financially, but it was worth it. Bob needed to reestablish a relationship with the boys, especially with the younger ones.

Whenever I have felt overwhelmed, I have drawn my strength and comfort from Philippians 4:13 and 19, "I can do everything through (Christ) who gives me strength," and "My God will meet all your needs according to his glorious riches in Christ Jesus." God has proven He will supply whatever I need.

ONE CHALLENGE AT A TIME
BY MARJORIE STREBE

Ever since I can remember, travel has been part of my life one way or another. My father is retired from the navy, so I never knew what it was like to stay in one place longer than three years. My dad was frequently away at sea and spent thirteen months in Vietnam. Sometimes it felt like I didn't have a father at all.

At twenty I joined the air force. Floyd and I met and married in England. Right after our wedding, Floyd went on temporary duty (TDY) for three weeks. When people asked where we were going on our honeymoon, Floyd joked that he was going to Italy, but I wasn't able to come along.

When our son, Toby, was born, I left the military, but Floyd remained in the air force as a jet mechanic, going TDY regularly. He'd be gone three weeks and home for two. Many days he'd call from work and say, "Hon, pack my bags. I leave in an hour."

As a civilian jet engine field service representative, Floyd's overseas trips lasted one to three months. Out-of-state trips lasted a couple of weeks. While Floyd was in Japan, a brick fell on our three-year-old daughter Michelle's hand and severed the tip of her finger. During this time frame, Michelle was diagnosed with William's Syndrome, a form of mental retardation that also manifests itself in hypochondria. She can fool the best of us into believing she is sick or injured. As part of her syndrome, Michelle has an obsession with rescue personnel—fire fighters, police officers, paramedics, etc. Her habitual impulse to dial 9-1-1 is a tremendous stress.

After a company layoff, Floyd went to work driving a semi-tractor-trailer rig for a few years. Initially he drove all over the country, and we hardly ever saw him. Then the Lord blessed him with a dedicated run so he could be home each weekend.

We got an 800 number, and Floyd could call home direct from anywhere in the United States. It was the cheapest way for us to communicate by telephone. He'd call just to talk to the children; they could discuss any problems with him. Sometimes Floyd would call late in the evening, after the children were in bed, to talk to me without interruption. We'd talk for an hour about problems I was facing with the children or in handling the finances—not my area of expertise. Some nights when I was struggling to balance the checkbook on the computer, Floyd would walk me through the process over the phone.

I am basically a happy-go-lucky person, but I missed Floyd's companionship and I didn't like being forced into the role of father as well as mother. One particular night, I felt so overwhelmed by the pressure of being a "single" parent that I cried to Floyd over the phone and begged him to quit his job and come home.

Floyd's second ten-day visit to the cardiac unit of the hospital ended his truck-driving career. Floyd has gone back to his previous trade as a jet engine field mechanic, minus benefits. I spend a lot of time at the airport, either picking him up or dropping him off. Assignments place him in another state for months at a time. During holidays and school breaks, the children and I may drive to visit Floyd. Sometimes the company runs out of work altogether. And though Floyd is home during these times, no work means no pay.

Problems increased as the three children got older. When Toby turned sixteen, he got his first job and his temporary driver's license. His attitude soured quickly. He decided school wasn't important and his mother didn't do anything but hassle him. Toby wanted to be with his dad, who didn't hassle him (because he was never home). Toby would complain to Floyd over the phone how mean and unfair I was.

Being able to look at the situation objectively, Floyd always offered good advice. (Sometimes I even thought Floyd was a little harsh.) Floyd told Toby if he didn't get his act together, he'd have to quit his job.

Floyd always backed me 100 percent, and that is vitally important to me. I quoted Floyd to the children:

"Toby, Dad said if your attitude doesn't improve, you will not be allowed to work."

"Mom, that's not fair!"

"Then take it up with your dad."

We have since restricted Toby's work to nonschool nights, and his grades have greatly improved.

How do I handle all my stress? One day I received a flash of insight. When Toby was fourteen, Floyd took him in the truck for two weeks. I arranged for a friend to keep the two girls, and I flew to Southern California to visit my parents for the first time in eight years. That relaxing vacation without the pressures and responsibilities of parenthood recharged my batteries.

One evening while talking with my mother, I suddenly felt incredibly overwhelmed by the circumstances. My mom asked how I managed to juggle all those problems at once and maintain my sanity. That was when it occurred to me that I usually didn't handle everything at once. As a situation arose, I'd handle that problem, and only that problem, the best I could at that moment.

Some situations required a decision before I could contact Floyd, so I went to my room, closed the door, and talked to God: "Lord, You know the situation, and I haven't a clue what to do. But I need to do it now. Give me wisdom. How do I handle this?"

Then I would sit quietly and listen. James 1:5 says, "If any of you lacks wisdom, he should ask God, who gives generously to all." In every instance, God has spoken to my heart and directed me, giving guidance and the wisdom I needed at that moment.

Finally, I make it a point never to dwell on a problem or worry about it. With my husband away, I don't need to get physically ill from worrying. When I am worrying I am not trusting God.

FROM JAMIE STREBE
FOURTEEN YEARS OLD

It is difficult with Dad gone all the time because I'm Daddy's girl. My dad and I have always had a good relationship. Over the last couple of years, I got rebellious. I felt my mom was unfair and I couldn't talk to her. I was uncooperative and mean to my sister, Michelle. I got rude and nasty.

Last summer I worked at a horse ranch cleaning stalls in exchange for riding lessons. My lessons were usually late and sometimes postponed. This situation stressed me out. It interfered with my homelife and chores. Mom always had something for me to do at home. I rarely had time for myself.

I hated my family. I hated school. I had no friends. I frequently made plans to run away. Once I even mentioned to a neighbor that I might jump out the window to break a few bones.

Two things happened that turned me around. First, my mom got me into counseling. That made me mad because I didn't want to be there. I refused to cooperate. But the counselor helped us learn how to communicate with each other. Second, Toby and I spent a couple of weeks with Dad. I felt completely stress-free. I missed the horses, but I didn't miss the stables. That was when I realized what the job was doing to me.

When I got home, before I even mentioned it, my mom perceived my dilemma. I enjoyed the horses but dreaded going back to work at the stables. We talked, and Mom advised me to give up the job. I was ready, but my employer was so demanding I was afraid to talk to her, so Mom went with me. I appreciated her support.

Today, my mother and I have a good relationship. We're friends. I like school, and I have several friends. But it didn't come easy. I had to do some changing. I'm glad I did.

STRATEGY

Parenting teenagers can be enjoyable. As young people bloom into adults, their own unique characteristics and sense of humor emerge.

Here are some practical ways these families have made this stage of family life rich and full.

For Husbands and Wives

- Expect to enjoy parenting your teenagers.
- Maintain consistent household and family standards. The rules concerning activities, dress, or associations do not change because a parent travels.
- Communicate. Pray together by phone when a spouse is out of town.
- Do not take each other for granted. Cherish the time you have together.
- Make extra efforts to keep the family together when individual schedules are pulling everyone in different directions. Plan family vacations, but also seek spontaneous ways to be together. Make family devotions and regular meals a priority.
- Develop common interests such as camping and sports activities. Be a part of your teen's world.
- Typically the wife and children feel angry, abandoned, and resentful about Dad's absence, growing more independent as they shoulder many of his responsibilities. When reentry issues surface, face them with a sense of humor and an attitude of turning lemons into lemonade.

For the Traveler

- Look for creative ways to stay close to your family. Lead family devotions when you are home.
- Listen to both sides of disputes between your wife and children. Always back your wife 100 percent. Be the "heavy" to maintain consistent discipline.
- Take a family member with you on business trips whenever possible.
- Keep spiritual health a daily priority no matter where you are. Model Christian values to your family, subordinates, peers, and superiors.

- Guard relationships with the opposite sex. Keep compliments professional, not personal.
- While out of town, find wholesome activities to fill your free time. Attend a church where you are. Develop relationships of accountability.
- Be open to making a job change if the Lord so prompts.

For the Fort Soldier

- Handle one crisis at a time.
- Keep your perspective. Determine to bring good out of your situation.
- Stay consistent with your parenting standards. This will provide emotional balance for you and your teenagers.
- Whenever possible, talk to your husband before making important decisions.
- Listen to your husband when he telephones home. Avoid spending the entire phone call complaining.
- Seek encouragement through prayer and Bible reading. Try journaling your prayers and thoughts.
- Continue family devotions while Dad is away.

For the Church and Others

- Be a supportive friend.
- Chat by phone every now and then.
- Help with transportation. Teenagers typically have busy schedules, each going in a different direction. Offer to pick up or drop teens off at their respective activities.
- Attend the teenagers' special events.
- Mentor a teenager through an age-appropriate Bible study.
- Teach a skill you know to a young person.
- Ask a young person to assist in church programs.

CHAPTER SIX

Military Families

If a man has recently married, he must not be sent to war or have any other duty laid on him. For one year he is to be free to stay at home and bring happiness to the wife he has married.

—DEUTERONOMY 24:5

S ITTING ON THE COUCH, *Kristy watched the tennis ball bounce back and forth across the television screen while she fed eight-week-old Ryan his bottle. Nearby, eighteen-month-old Alec played with toys.*

The Wimbledon tennis court was briefly intercepted by the face of an announcer with curly dark hair. Each time the announcer appeared, Alec ran to touch the television screen. "Daddy!" he proclaimed. "Daddy! Daddy!"

Ryan emptied his bottle as Kristy checked the clock. Time to go to church. Switching off the television, Kristy gathered Ryan and the baby things and headed for the car with Alec toddling beside her.

As Kristy settled Ryan in his car seat, Alec spotted a uniformed man walking past their house. "Daddy!" Alec called, his little legs running after the sailor. Alec nearly caught up with his target when the sailor realized he was being followed. He squatted to Alec's level and the toddler threw himself into the stranger's arms. The serviceman caught Alec and stood. Kristy quickly came to get her son.

With a big smile, the sailor gave Alec a man-size hug, then turned to Kristy. "Your husband is deployed," he stated matter-of-factly.

"Yes," Kristy sighed as the sailor passed Alec into her arms. "Todd is deployed."

———

For military personnel, travel is part of the job description and has been since the first army was formed. Likewise, travel is nothing new for the serviceman's family; they have lived this lifestyle years before most of the rest of us.

HARDER THAN YOU CAN IMAGINE
KRISTY AND TODD NEAL'S STORY

Everything is new for Kristy and Todd Neal. Their marriage is new, their home is new, parenthood is new, and the traveling life of the military family is new.

Todd works in data systems aboard the world's largest ship, the USS *Abraham Lincoln*. Only a few years old, the aircraft carrier houses the latest in technology as well as five thousand crew members at a time.

While stationed at California's historic Mare Island Naval Base, Todd married Kristy, whom he met at church. They scheduled their wedding during a short period when Todd was in port. The newlyweds honeymooned at their own rented cottage because what they both wanted most was to be "home" together. Shortly after Todd shipped out, Kristy telegraphed the news that he was to be a daddy. Todd observed the pregnancy only through photos Kristy mailed to him. Todd arrived home just in time for Alec's birth.

Seven months later, Kristy and Todd knew they were expecting again. Within weeks after Ryan's birth, Todd left for another six months at sea. Kristy's emotions raced between happiness over her newborn and depression over Todd's lengthy deployment. She grieved over how much of Ryan's short babyhood her husband would miss, and struggled with the enormous job of parenting a toddler and a baby alone.

Living on base, Kristy was far away from her home church and the support of her parents and sister. One morning Alec found a tube of bright red lipstick and scribbled all over the living room wall. Kristy's pent-up tension erupted. "I'm gonna kill you!" she screamed. "I wish I'd never had you."

Kristy related, "I shouldn't have said it. Someone overheard me and turned me in to Child Protective Services. An officer came to my door to see if I was abusing my child. I wish, instead of turning me in, that neighbor would have come over to see if I needed help.

"The hard parts are harder than you can imagine," Kristy confessed. "I pray all day. I pray simple prayers: *Every day I look to You to be the strength of my life. Be the strength of my life. Jesus loves me this I know because the Bible tell me so.* My prayers are less fancy and more honest than before. Now they sound like life: *God, why did You let this happen?*

Married two years, Kristy and Todd haven't seen each other much. To keep Todd involved with the family while he is deployed, Kristy writes to him every day. "Some days I just write, 'Honey, I'm too tired. I'll write tomorrow and tell you all about it.' I send Todd a package once a week with cassettes of the kids talking, and fast-food children's meal prizes wrapped in a ton of tape, like a kid would do. I write all over the back of the photos I send and include a letter from Alec's point of view written with my left hand. Alec colors on all my letters. Once I took a picture of Alec with his crayons and sent it with the letter he colored. Todd laminated the letter and taped it above his bunk."

Though less frequent at first, Todd's letters are a lifeline for Kristy. During his last deployment, fifty days went by without a letter from Todd. "I wrote to him and said, if you still love us, you better write because you are a part of this family and you have a responsibility to us," Kristy recalled. "I've gotten a letter every day since. I told him it didn't matter if he only gave me the menu for dinner, I just needed him to communicate."

She continued, "When Todd's away, I play my music box with the song 'Somewhere Out There.' Todd thinks I torture myself, which I do, but sometimes it just feels good. I wear his clothes just to see them in the wash. During his first deployment, I went for months without hugging another person. Now I can cuddle the children."

Prior to Todd's deployment to the Middle East, Kristy videotaped

Todd reading Alec's favorite storybooks. The video begins with Todd holding up a storybook and saying, "Now Alec, go and get this book." Daddy reads the story while Alec follows the pictures.

The homecoming is what the Neal family all look forward to. "When Todd came home last time, I was surprised that I had totally forgotten how warm his lips are," Kristy said. "There is nothing like that day at the pier when that ship comes in and he's up there on deck and I'm down on the pier and I have to wait until he comes down that ramp. I have earned that moment, and it's unbelievable. There is this place on his chest where my cheek just fits and when my cheek is there, *I'm* home."

Preparing for Widowhood
Kathy and Jeff Arnette's Story

Kathy and Jeff Arnette had been married four years when the Gulf War broke out. A field medic, Jeff had previously enlisted with the National Guard to complete his medical training. Based in Oklahoma, Jeff's unit served essentially as a mobile emergency room (ER) for the military.

Only thirty days remained of Jeff's enlistment when the phone rang at 3:00 A.M. on November 11, 1990. The code words "Raging Bull" activated Jeff's unit. All personnel were to report for duty by 11:00 A.M. for up to four years of service.

For the next month, Sergeant Arnette worked to ready the unit for deployment to the Middle East. In addition, Jeff had to complete his will, secure power of attorney, and put all his personal matters in order in case he didn't return home alive. In December, the 145th medical unit boarded a plane for the other side of the world. Jeff left behind his wife and sons, two-year-old Michael and eight-month-old Brandon.

"I looked at the worst-case scenario," Kathy recalled. "I was preparing myself for widowhood and trying to avoid the constant news coverage. All we were hearing was doomsday talk about chemical weapons. I wondered if I was causing this hardship because I had been demanding life my way. But it was wartime, and in retrospect it was short and quick."

The day before Jeff left for Saudi Arabia, the family car died. Not only did Jeff lack the time to fix the problem, he began distancing himself emotionally. "My only thoughts were of chemical warfare and overseeing the platoon's readiness. Something had to get in line," he related. "I knew our parents and church were there, so Kathy would not be alone."

An anonymous church member gave Kathy $1,500 for a car, and Kathy was especially pleased when the car she purchased left her with $150 to tithe back to the Lord. "I still don't know who gave us that money," she noted. "But I pray for them all the time, that God would bless them."

Financial problems were a heavy burden for Kathy during the six months Jeff was away. No paycheck from Jeff's regular job cut the family's income in half. Sometimes people would invite Kathy and the boys for dinner, but often Kathy didn't have enough gas in the car to get there. "It seemed to take me a minimum of two hours to get us all cleaned up, dressed, and out of the house," Kathy explained. "I tried, but getting everybody ready, then protecting our hosts' knickknacks, and trying to feed three people was too exhausting."

Before long, Kathy realized she was in real trouble. "The baby was colicky, and I hadn't gotten any sleep," she said. "Once a friend picked up my active two-year-old so he could play at her house for a couple of hours. That was so wonderful! I will always remember her ministry to me. Another day two friends brought some fast food and talked to me while I played on the floor with the children. At that time, my sweet, curious, rowdy two-year-old couldn't be trusted out of my sight. Not having to cook dinner (I could barely afford food) and having an adult to talk to were blessings I will never forget."

Kathy and Jeff communicated mostly by phone. Servicemen would travel miles to phone centers and stand in line to call home. "There were fifteen thousand men and three phone sites of about one hundred and fifty phones," Jeff said. "The best time was at odd hours, but often the phone would go dead while we were talking."

Jeff lived with constant danger. "We were the first unit into combat and the last out," Jeff reported. "We spent three days treating prisoners of war (POWs) with M16 rifles pointed at us. But the first time I felt completely powerless as a husband was when I called home and Kathy's first words were, 'I'm all right.' She told me she had been robbed at gunpoint at an ATM. That's when it hit me there was nothing I could do."

Jeff struggled spiritually during the Gulf War. "I had thought I would get closer to God, but it didn't happen that way," he admitted. "We began a Bible study, but that petered out. Moral standards were at an all-time low. Male and female military personnel cohabited in close quarters, fueling inappropriate emotional and physical relationships. Christians were ordered to keep a lid on their faith and store Bibles out of sight."

"It was a blurry time when my husband was gone," Kathy described. "I continued to work at my church—the only time I could talk in full sentences to other adults—while other sweet sisters cared for my children. I also continued to have house church meetings at my home, but I did myself in trying to keep the house in order. I wish I had been relaxed or secure enough to leave the dinner dishes or the floor dirty."

Kathy listed helpful hints she learned. "It is so important to stay in fellowship. Tell people when you are in over your head. God gave me wisdom, but the practical stuff came from the church body and from friends."

Jeff's return home presented a new challenge for the Arnettes. "I felt I'd come home to a new family," Jeff recalled. "Physically they had all changed a lot. I had stepped out of time in December and stepped back in May. I left a baby but came home to a toddler. I had missed Brandon's first words, his first steps, his first everything. I knew I couldn't make up that time or replace it. I felt robbed. I had an aggressive, defiant, angry attitude when I came back."

A friend eased the adjustment period for the Arnettes by caring for the children the first forty-eight hours Jeff was home. "We needed to set a plan for me to get reacquainted with the children and to gradually be able to discipline them," Jeff explained.

"Our experience taught us to have compassion on other people," Kathy said. "When we see others who are stressed out, we take food over or take their children to the park for a while. It's important for the church to come alongside and help bear one another's burdens. I ask what I can do, and if they say 'nothing,' I respond, 'No, I'm going to do something. What do you need? I'll call back later or tomorrow and let you think it over.' For us it mattered that people cared."

Kathy concluded, "I found myself thinking, *Why, God?* I realized that when we have life easy we fall in love with life and out of longing for the presence of the Lord. Once you get to the other side of tough times, you say, 'Thank you, God! What kind of a person would I be if You had left me where I was?' Hard times develop godly character. James 1:2–4 says, 'Consider it pure joy, my brothers, whenever you face trials of many kinds, because you know that the testing of your faith develops perseverance. Perseverance must finish its work so that you may be mature and complete, not lacking anything.' Be open and tender before God to receive all He desires to teach you."

STEADY STEAMERS
MARY AND TOM THOMPSON'S STORY

"How many of you have seen *The Hunt for Red October*?" Tom referred to the award-winning film as he spoke to a roomful of teens for Career Day. They had all seen the movie.

"Well," Tom summarized, "that's what I do."

Career military, Tom Thompson advanced from executive officer of ballistic missile submarine USS *Nevada* to captain of the fast-attack nuclear submarine USS *Pintado*. He has sailed the world's oceans and visited exotic ports. As aide-de-camp to U.S. Strategic Command, Tom has flown to foreign countries and frequented high-power strategic meetings.

Tom and Mary Thompson are self-described "steady steamers." Far more interested in people than titles or positions, Tom and Mary have four children, from preschooler to married daughter, and have made fifteen moves in twenty years of marriage. Mary is a nurse, Bible study leader, and homeschooling mother. A stay-at-home mother since their first child was born, she has been instrumental in founding Bible studies and statewide Nurses for Life organizations in a number of states. "I keep my interests from taking my focus. My first focus is the children, our marriage, and our home," Mary said.

Assigned to the ballistic missile sub, Tom's schedule was a regular three months at sea, three months in port. Surprisingly, in those first thirteen years Tom was home for Thanksgiving and Christmas and the births of their first two children. Promoted to executive officer of the USS *Nevada*, Tom left port one week before their third daughter was born. As a toddler, Beka recognized her daddy's photo more readily than the three-dimensional model when the family gathered on the pier to greet the incoming submarine. "I kept pointing to my identification photo on my badge, then pointing to my face and telling her, "Look, it's Daddy, Daddy," Tom said.

Once the submarine submerged, contact between crew members and their families was extremely limited. Tom could contact his family when the ship docked. Mary could send one-way family grams, which were received when the ship surfaced to receive transmissions. "I could send up to one family gram a week," Mary noted. "They could only be fifty words in length, so it was important to make each word count. I began each family gram with Scripture, and the message transferred over fleet radio. When Tom submerged, there was a long silence for months. I didn't know what was happening in his life. So I'd read the Bible, looking for the right Scripture to send Tom. One time Proverbs 23:7a [KJV], jumped out: 'For as he thinketh in his heart, so is he.' After he got home, I was unpacking Tom's seabag and found this wrinkled family gram. Having made a mistake he would not let himself forget, Tom was having a hard time when this family gram arrived. He had carried my message in his pocket so long it looked like parchment."

Despite long absences, communication remained a vital link between Mary and Tom. "I kept a journal of daily writings. I mailed a packet every ten days," Mary outlined. Mary included spiritual insights and devotional thoughts, as well as the day-to-day news of the family. Tom packed a blank stenographer's notebook to record his days. "He gave the notebook to me when he got back. That proved the most useful thing we ever did, because he won't remember what he did five months ago," she said.

With Tom at sea, Mary's main support came from her church and the other wives of men on Tom's ship. The ship's crew numbered one hundred forty men, and about eighty were married. When the ship sailed, some wives returned home to stay with extended family. The rest remained to set up housekeeping at the submarine's home port.

"The more senior Tom got, the more responsibility I felt," Mary described. "People's children got seriously ill, they had family traumas and crises. For the Christian there is the solid foundation in the Lord, but for the nonbeliever it's tough. It's hard for people who have not experienced this kind of separation to understand what it's like. You get tired. You just want it to be over. That's when you need someone who says, 'Hey, why don't you come over for dinner.' And then you feel refreshed and ready to go again."

Halfway Night is a traditional celebration for the wives, marking the day deployment is half over. Mary recalled, "One trip we had the guys write a note their wives would receive on Halfway Night. That night was a big occasion, with valet parking and waiters. A couple of us wives parked the cars and then changed our clothes to be waiters. Dinner was at our house, so we put up a sign and called it the Executive Inn because Tom was the Executive Officer (XO). It was all formal dress, and the notes were given with dessert. There were some tears and some good laughs."

The Thompson children also celebrated the halfway point in their father's trips. With a minimum of planning ahead, each child received a gift all the more special because of Tom's personal touch. Tom arranged for the florist to deliver balloons on Valentine's Day. He wrote out cards ahead of time to be given to the children on special occasions.

"The pressure on the guys is intense the weeks before shipping out," Mary related. "It is physically impossible to do everything. Many of us women have read all the books, we know what men are supposed to do. But we must remember we are their helpmeets. I'm home with the children all the time. I share my observations about the children with Tom, and Tom listens. Together we develop a plan, and I help him carry the responsibility he has before God. To do otherwise would rob our children of knowing their father to be as wonderful as I know him to be."

Before Tom's departure, Mary and the children write and date cards for Tom to read throughout his trip. "I also asked ten godly men in our church to write Tom a letter," Mary shared. "Some of the letters were about spiritual things, some were encouragements. As the captain, Tom didn't have an older man on ship to fellowship with. Similarly, on his last deployment as an executive officer, I arranged for other commanders to write letters giving Tom their input on command. The commanders gave their letters to me; I dated and packed them. The men from church and the men in the military wanted to do something. They appreciated being asked to write a letter, and Tom appreciated those letters."

Though Mary knows how tough it can be for the wife who waits for her husband to return, she has a lasting memory of the day she got a taste of what the separation felt like for Tom. "Inevitably when Tom leaves, the washer goes, the car breaks down," she listed, "but it's hard for him too." While serving as a navigator, Tom's sub docked at Ft. Lauderdale, Florida. Mary arranged for someone to care for the children so she could spend five days with Tom.

"We were having prayer time together like we do each morning, and I just broke down. I told Tom, 'I'm sorry. I love you, I want to be with you, but I miss those little guys so much.' I realized what a step of faith it is for Tom to walk away, to slice himself off from all he loves the most. I found I have the better deal. The washer can be fixed, but I'm with the ones I love the most. I came to appreciate the need for family grams and to always meet Tom on the pier, even if he's only been away a few days."

Tom and Mary make every effort to keep the family together. "We went with Tom when he went to PCO school, even though it was only for three months. Too often families mistakenly preserve ties with the children's peers but don't even consider the serious effects of breaking family ties. It's more important for the children to have that family tie, to be together with their father," Mary emphasized.

At home, Tom strives to do things with his family. "Rather than watch football, work out, or read, the time is better spent with the children and Mary," he said. "It's a matter of self-control. When I'm traveling, I have a lot of time alone to study my Bible. At home, I study early in the morning while everyone else is still in bed so I'm not taking time from the family. My priorities are time in Scripture and time with family."

Mary echoed, "We maintain our commitment to the Lord and our commitment to our marriage. To avoid appearances of evil, I don't have men friends over when Tom is away, and Tom arranges his meetings with friends in ports without the appearance of impropriety. Neither of us go the Officer's Club just to sit around with the music and single people. We avoid places that could get us into trouble."

"People have different temperaments," Tom observed. "Mary has been the glue that has kept it all together for us. If she had needed more of me than she has, it would have been a lot harder. Mary has learned to make the shift. When I leave, it's her problem. When I come back, she steps back, even though she is still the one who makes things click around here. Major decisions and discipline are all done through me, with me as the major authority. Mary and I sit down with the children and explain what is expected and how things run. The children are very much aware that Mary and I are together in our decisions and actions, so there won't be any playing one parent against another to get what they want. We grow closer together so it's harder for me to go, but it doesn't take as long for me to step back in as part of the house."

"It's not an easy lifestyle," Mary said. "But we know this is what God has called us to do."

EPILOGUE

After twenty-two years in the military, Tom retired from the navy. He now serves as Officer Christian Fellowship Staff Representative at the U.S. Naval Academy.

"My job is to work with midshipmen, building their faith in Jesus

Christ and teaching them how to walk by faith as naval officers."

"This is a parachurch ministry," Mary described. "We prepare young men and women in the military, teaching them to do what we did for twenty-two years. It's a glove fit."

With their oldest child in college, one in high school, and two in the elementary grades, the Thompson family greeted the arrival of baby Grace with great joy.

STRATEGY

It doesn't have to be the end of the world when your spouse travels to the ends of the world. Military families often experience the double challenge of having Dad away on duty while his family tries to acclimate to a new area.

For Husbands and Wives

- Be trustworthy, respectable, and honorable. Avoid places that could get you in trouble. Don't let jealousy be a wedge between you.
- Celebrate anniversaries, birthdays, and other holidays. If you will be apart on a significant date, arrange for a gift or card that can be opened on that day.
- Keep the family together whenever possible. Relocate if necessary. Family ties are more important than ties with peers.
- Sit down together with the children and explain your home's discipline policy so they know what to expect. Be united in your parenting; support each other in your decisions.
- Organize a maintenance schedule for cars, yard work, appliances, and other household needs so the wife can expedite service at the proper time. Many companies, from propane suppliers to car dealers, offer systematic maintenance agreements.
- After being away for an extended time, allow some flexibility as Dad transitions back into the family. Create a plan to get

reacquainted. Talk a lot—gently—without putting one another on the defensive.

- Discipline yourself to do Bible study, even if you don't feel like it.

For the Traveler

- Maintain your position as the major authority in the family. Lead regular family devotions when you are home, and encourage your family to continue the devotions you initiated while you are away.
- Be a student of your wife and children. Seek to know them and their unique personalities. When home, spend time with them.
- Listen to your wife's observations about the children. She is your eyes and ears despite the days and miles between you.
- Communicate with your family, even if it's only to tell them what you had for dinner. Your wife and children need to hear from you. Overseas travel can make telephone communication difficult, but computer e-mail is frequently more accessible and economical.
- Post photos of your family in your work space.
- Before deployment, make audiocassettes and videos of you reading favorite stories to the children.
- Finish important household projects before leaving on a trip.
- When you return, give Mom time to rest and get some deep, uninterrupted sleep. She's been on duty on the home front for a long time.

For the Fort Soldier

- Allow Dad to maintain his place as the major authority in the family.
- Pray about everything and read your Bible regularly. Study the Bible with your children; read Bible stories to your little ones.
- Keep your family as your top priority.
- Have photos of Dad around the home.
- Utilize family grams, mail, e-mail, and any other available mode of communication to stay in touch with your husband. Encourage him with Scripture.
- Send photos, the children's artwork, audiocassettes, inspirational

books, and small treats to your husband.

- Relax and maintain a sense of humor.
- Sleep when your children sleep so you are rested.
- Stay in fellowship with other believers. Develop friendships with women in the same situation. Seek out Christian support groups such as Moms In Touch (P.O. Box 1163, Poway, CA 92064).
- Tell people when you need help. Be specific about your needs when someone offers assistance.
- Don't be afraid of a challenge. If you want to go someplace, go, even if you can't find someone to go with you.
- Celebrate Halfway Night.
- Meet your husband when he comes home. Be on the dock or at the base, even if he has only been away a few days.

For the Church and Others

- Military families are frequently stationed long distances from family and friends. Holidays and weekends can be especially lonely. Invite them over.
- Pray for them often. Write to the husband when he is away. He needs encouraging fellowship too.
- Beware of judging appearances. Rather than assuming the worst about a family, ask how they are doing. Drop by and see how they are managing. Offer to help in specific ways. Don't take "no" for an answer.
- Play with the children so Mom can get a break, take a nap, or run errands.
- Drop off a meal; even fast food will be a blessing. Fill the gas tank or service the car if finances are a problem. Give gift certificates for long-distance phone calls.
- Care for the children when Dad comes home so husband and wife can spend some much-needed alone time together.

CHAPTER SEVEN

Travel and Ministry

> Then Jesus came to them and said, "All authority in heaven and on
> earth has been given to me. Therefore go and make disciples of all
> nations, baptizing them in the name of the Father and of the Son and
> of the Holy Spirit, and teaching them to obey everything
> I have commanded you. And surely I am with you always,
> to the very end of the age."
>
> —MATTHEW 28:18–20

I'VE SPENT A LOT OF TIME THIS FALL ON THE ROAD—*"giving blood" in
the state of California for school choice and in the state of Washington
for a serious criminal law. It was worth the time, but it was time away from
home—and I could tell.*

*"I was in California on a Wednesday, Thursday, Friday, and Saturday.
I was scheduled to fly back Sunday for dinner in Washington with Elayne
and the boys, and then fly back to California on Monday. So on Saturday,
in Los Angeles, I thought it might make more sense to stay, so I called home.
I didn't get Elayne, I didn't get John. I got Joe, my four-year-old.*

I said, "Hi, Joe, how ya' doin'?"

He said, "Fine."

I said, "What's new?"

"Nothin'."

"How's Mom?"

"Fine."

"How's your brother?"

"Fine."

"How are your friends?"

"Fine."

We had this kind of conversation for five minutes, and then in the middle of it Joe said, "Who's calling, please?"

And I said, "It's your Daddy."

"You want to speak to Mom?"

I said, "No, just tell Mom I'll be home tomorrow night for dinner."

—Dr. William J. Bennett
   author and co-director of Empower America (from his 1994
   keynote speech for the twentieth anniversary of the Heritage
   Foundation)

———————

For some families travel is part of their calling, the necessary vehicle to take the Gospel into all the world. Does the calling make the travel lifestyle any easier for the family? What can other families learn from their experiences?

ONE IN MARRIAGE AND IN MINISTRY
BY AMANDA McKEEHAN

I always dreamed I would marry a man who had a nine-to-five job and live no more than two miles from my parents. I thought my children would go to my alma mater, and I would go grocery shopping with my mother every Wednesday. That's why I cried at my bridal shower. I was scared to death of moving from my home in Jamaica to a lifestyle in America that was completely opposite my dream. I knew I couldn't live without Toby, but I was scared of what life was going to be like with him.

My husband, Toby, performs with the Christian music group dc Talk. They seek to produce music that is biblically solid and uplifting to the Lord, yet music young people can proudly play for their non-Christian friends.

Toby's demanding schedule includes not only performing but also producing, promoting, writing, and partnership responsibilities in record and management companies. His job takes him all over the world and keeps him away from home 60 percent of the year. I don't tour with Toby for the same reason other wives don't sit at their husband's desk all day while their husband is working.

Toby and I dated for five and a half years before we got married, so I knew what I was getting into. I had seen dc Talk grow and understood what it meant to share my husband with his fans and his job. But understanding does not make it easy and definitely does not take away the loneliness. The first few months of our marriage I felt so alone. I would lock myself in the closet and cry because I didn't want Toby to see how upset I was that he was leaving again. I wondered why I had ever married this man if I was going to be alone anyway.

I would have drowned in self-pity had it not been for my personal time alone with the Lord. God showed me that Toby's love was like the cherry on top of an ice cream sundae. The Lord's love was the ice cream, the sauce, the whipped cream, and the nuts. The love I had thought was so big was actually very small—just a cherry in comparison to what the Lord had to offer. The Lord's love could overflow in me. His love could satisfy my needs. There was no end to Him and He was never out of reach or too far away.

Such a simple illustration, but it made sense to me. I realized that Toby's love was a beautiful hand-picked gift from God, but compared to all the other things in a sundae, it was not very filling. Slowly I began to stop expecting my needs to be filled in the cherry, and I started letting the immensity of the Lord's love fill me. How precious of the Lord to show me the way to fulfillment!

In those quiet times with the Lord I found my strength and contentment. God answered my questions and quieted my fears. Now one of the upsides to Toby's traveling is the intimacy that I have with the Lord when Toby is gone.

dc Talk has a pastor who travels with them, and his wife, Celeste, is one of my dearest friends. Years ago she and I realized that the Lord wanted us to start a ministry to wives whose husbands were on the road with the dc Talk tour. We began with a small group of women, including the wives of the band members, the road crew, the opening acts—any woman who was left alone at home because of the dc Talk tour. Celeste and I took turns leading the group, sharing what the Lord was teaching us in our own personal lives.

We had all left our extended families behind and moved to Nashville. Most of us were newlyweds, and we had many fears and questions. It was difficult for us to accept that it was the Lord's will for our husbands to travel so much.

How, as husband and wife, were we supposed to become one when we were never together? We were sharing our lives more with our friends than with our mates. As far as the human eye could see, we were growing more apart than together.

But in one of our meetings the Lord taught us that when He makes two people one, it is a supernatural act not constrained by distance or lack of communication. I will never forget that night because such a peace came over us all as we submitted our relationships to the power of the Lord. We prayed that the Lord, by His miraculous power, would make us one with our husbands in spirit, soul, and mind. It was a turning point for the women.

The Lord showed us that we needed to partner with our husbands' ministries in prayer. God gave us a dramatic picture of our men on the spiritual battlefield, fighting and struggling to keep going, while we enjoyed the safety and peace of our homes. Often our husbands' days were so busy they didn't have quiet time to pray for various issues. We saw we could help them by praying specifically and faithfully for their needs.

Amazingly, as we began to pray for our men, *our* attitudes changed toward their traveling. As we saw our husbands out there touching young people's lives for Christ, we felt more willing to let them go. Most important, as we took on the ministry in prayer, our marriages and the organization as a whole grew in oneness and unity.

As the size of the tour has grown, so has our women's group. On a recent tour, the guys did sixty shows in ninety days. Including rehearsals, they were gone for the better part of four months. At the "end of the tour" party, we reviewed how the tour went. Every couple agreed the Lord had brought them closer together while we were apart.

I wish I could share all the answers that the Lord has provided for my fears, loneliness, and inability to run the house on my own. I wish I could list all the promises He has shown me in His Word. I can only say I enjoy much more security and love than I dreamed possible. I still have a long road to walk, but Philippians 4:12–13 expresses how I am growing: I have learned the secret of being content in any and every situation, whether well fed or hungry, whether living in plenty or in want. I can do all things through Christ who gives me strength.

My personal time alone with Jesus Christ is the strength of my happiness. There isn't a special method or formula for dealing with a traveling husband, but it can be done victoriously through Jesus Christ. A personal relationship with Jesus Christ is the daily answer to loneliness, the way to turn a difficult lifestyle into a healthy, productive one.

BOOT CAMP ON THE ROAD
RICHARD "LITTLE BEAR" WHEELER'S STORY

As an evangelist historian, my family and I spent the early years of our ministry in a twenty-four-foot motor home. Imagine conducting the activities of four people in such a small spot. When little Joshua was born, we used the bathtub as his cradle.

Traveling extensively in those early days, my wife, Marilyn, longed for roots that her earlier upbringing had provided. During Marilyn's quiet time, rocking our daughter, Aimee, in an unfamiliar church nursery, she wondered how she could be "like a tree planted by streams of water, which yields its fruit in season" (Psalm 1:3) if she wasn't rooted on the home front. The Lord, the Vinedresser, impressed on her heart that it wasn't necessary to be physically rooted in one location to yield spiritual fruit, but that wherever He would lead, from one state to another, from one city to another, she could think of herself as a potted plant being moved from one place to another. As long as she was watered by His living water (John 4:10–14), she would still yield fruit in due season. That spoke to Marilyn's craving for security. It was the turning point in her life.

We went through boot camp on the road. God has graduated us

from boot camp and given us a home. Marilyn has put down roots and feels more effective as a home educator, wife, and mother. Today I travel by plane, and Marilyn remains at home. While I'm traveling, Marilyn has three avenues of support: first, the Lord; second, my prayers; and third, the support of friends and the local church.

I travel throughout the United States. When I am in town, my office is in our home so I am able to be part of my children's lives. This is one of the reasons we home-educate. Time is tight. I can barely keep the ministry afloat with the responsibilities that I have at home, in the office, and on the road. I balance my travel schedule with time off for my family.

We travel as a family a few times each year. Our three children have made friends throughout the nation, and have become resilient as a result of the traveling. They've learned to bounce from home to home, place to place, sleep where ever they can lay their heads—at all hours—and eat whatever is set before them. They can function in the midst of confusion. Marilyn finds refuge in the Lord in morning devotions. Marilyn's life verse is, "Being confident of this, that he who began a good work in you will carry it on to completion until the day of Christ Jesus" (Phil. 1:6). My life verse has been the classic Proverbs 3:5–6: "Trust in the Lord with all your heart and lean not on your own understanding; in all your ways acknowledge him, and he will make your paths straight." This has been the foundation of our marriage and ministry.

It's important that men who travel continue to be the leader in the home, to be spiritually strong, sound in doctrine, and full of the strength of the Lord, because you cannot impart to your children what you do not yourself possess.

In my experience, I have found most men in America today go to work, come home exhausted, and do little except read the paper, watch television, or engage in sports. Rarely equipped to debate, stand firm, and be outspoken in the cause of righteousness, they often fall prey to entertainment, which actually weakens their spiritual strength. Our strength must be found in the Scriptures, not television, videos, movies, or other entertainment that encourages poor judgment.

I encourage men to read the Bible daily, and to spend time each day interceding in prayer for their family and their nation. There is no substitute for knowing God's Word, being well-educated, and reading quality books. Just as Nehemiah posted a watchman on the wall, men today must be on guard so that the spiritual walls around our homes and families will not be broken down.

TAKING THE GOSPEL INTO ALL THE WORLD
PAT AND LUIS PALAU'S STORY

Pat and Luis Palau have traveled the globe for more than three decades, successfully raised four sons, and welcomed grandchildren. Not only have they survived this challenge, they have thrived as a family.

A native of Argentina, Luis met Pat while both were students at Multnomah Bible College in Portland, Oregon. Pat shared Luis's heart for evangelism, and after their marriage, the two traveled to South America as missionary/evangelists with Overseas Crusades (now OC International). Though the Luis Palau Evangelistic Team (formed in 1967) initially focused their ministry in Latin America, crusade invitations have taken them to Europe and Asia, places as diverse as Auckland and Zurich, Leningrad and Singapore, Bucharest and Hong Kong. Luis has preached to hundreds of millions of people—face-to-face and via radio and television broadcasts. From the first crusade in 1966 to the present, more than half a million people have made public commitments of faith to Jesus Christ.

"Nothing is more important than leading souls into the eternal kingdom," Luis stated. "This is the primary duty of every Christian." The Luis Palau Evangelistic Association's vision is to preach the Gospel, mobilize the church, and influence church leadership. That vision has required worldwide travel.

Pat reflects on the thirty-plus years her family has lived the travel lifestyle:

Luis's career choice didn't leave me with many models. I traveled some with Luis the first year we were married but wasn't prepared for the deep loneliness I experienced when we moved overseas—first to Costa Rica when our twins, Kevin and Keith, were less than a year old, then to Colombia, where Andrew was born, and finally to Mexico, where I gave birth to Stephen.

Those preschool years were particularly exhausting, both physically and emotionally. Often Luis would be in another country, and no one knew I needed and wanted help. For example, I didn't learn to drive until I was thirty-five years old. I had a traveling husband and a car parked in my driveway, but I could not get anywhere unless I could walk there with four little people.

When our children were small, they seemed to mirror my emotions. When I was happy, my boys were emotionally secure. The opposite was also true. One morning in Colombia, when Luis was on a trip, we were listening to him speak on the radio. The boys began to whine. They missed Daddy. So did I!

From ages six to twelve, our sons picked on each other, and I tried not to lose my cool. That was the period when I most missed Luis's presence and perspective. At least I liked the same sports the boys did, so we had a lot of fun.

I like to read, and I read to my kids for hours. I challenged myself mentally, and during that time overseas I read everything I could, including missionary biographies. Those people who planted the church suffered sacrifices we will never understand. I also taught myself to knit—a little thing I still do.

Technology has advanced greatly since we first began our work overseas. When Luis was speaking at crusades in Peru, for example, the phones didn't always function. Calls from Luis simply would not come through. Airplanes flew less frequently as well. Though Luis planned to be away for two weeks, lack of an outgoing flight or airline delays often detained him longer. It was a relief when flights became more regular and dependable.

In 1971 we moved the family and ministry to Portland, Oregon. With crusade invitations beginning to come from Europe, we needed a more stable place to raise our family. Having grown up in Portland,

I was surrounded by my parents, relatives, and childhood friends. Until ten years ago, I sat under the same pastoral team I knew as a child. In times of crisis, I went to them for help. My pastor's wife seemed to know my needs before I did.

Today my children and grandchildren live nearby and visit often, so I am never alone. Sometimes I accompany Luis and help him. Three of our four sons have joined their father in ministry. They and their families are second-generation Palaus experiencing the travel lifestyle. My heart goes out to my daughters-in-law, but at least I can say I understand. When the men are gone, we women do a lot of fun things together, and they bring the grandchildren to visit.

I've probably spent one-third of our married life by myself, but I've learned to come to terms with it. Over the years I've leaned on the promise in Scripture that God will never leave us. In fact, that's the last promise Jesus made. This is not a theory, but a fact. The reality of God's presence has helped me quit keeping track of how much Luis is away. I've stopped fighting the travel issue. I've ceased keeping score. Score-keeping is the antithesis of the Gospel's definition of grace. The world's "balance of power" concept, with Mom doing only her 50 percent, is not biblical.

The Bible never promised life would be fair. In the Andes, Luis preached until he was literally blue due to the high altitude. He slept in the same clothes for three weeks. He was constantly cold. At home in Cali, Colombia, the kids had been deathly sick, and I was getting no sleep. Each of us could have competed for a "suffering" medal. But we couldn't truly imagine how the other felt.

We women spend too much of our time wishing our husbands understood. We need to lighten up. We would not expect this of any other person. God is with us always. I can't ask from Luis what only God can give—understanding. When we make a choice to put the Lord first, then the rest falls into place eventually.

Luis and I made conscious decisions to keep our marriage strong. From the beginning, we've built safeguards around our marriage. I like the book *Hedges* by Jerry Jenkins. Luis and I lived those principles even before the book was written. Today, stories of "come-ons" at airports, in hotels, or on planes are commonplace. Luis and I show a cool propriety if someone makes an inappropriate suggestion or behaves improperly toward us.

As a safeguard, Luis never travels alone. He is accompanied by a team associate, one of our sons, or me. One of the most trying times for us was when I was diagnosed with cancer and spent more than two years in chemotherapy. At the time, we had three adolescents and a ten-year-old, so Luis cut way back on his travel to spend more time at home.

We've established safeguards around our family as well. For instance, four times during the Reagan years, Luis was invited to the White House. Although visiting with the president would have been personally enriching, it cut into family time.

There are trade-offs. Luis opted not to spend time "with the guys" or pursue golf, which he enjoyed. We prefer to spend all the time possible with our family. When we played, it was with our kids.

We encourage our staff to invest money and time on family fun and trips. We encourage each wife to take a ministry trip every year with her husband. Then she knows why she is sacrificing, and she feels part of the ministry.

We kept our sons in a place of high priority. They deserve to have their needs met. We tried not to miss the children's major events, and when possible, we took our sons along on ministry trips that were suitable and appealed to them. One spring break we did a television and radio ministry in Puerto Rico. Our sons saw Europe from the back of a van. As a benefit of our travels together, they understand different cultures and languages.

We also had a few near disasters on our trips. Once a woman who accompanied us on a trip to Europe lost the children in a town. We finally sent the dog out and he found them.

We've teased each other a lot, but never when it would hurt another. Some of our funniest times were the nightmare situations. Luis is a city person, and he still repents for some of our camping experiences. On one vacation it took us twenty-four hours to get the borrowed mobile home level. It rained the whole trip, so we played games crammed together in our home on wheels. To top it off, the waste sanitation tank fell off.

During our twenty-six years of raising children, Luis probably spent as much or more time with his sons than he would have if he'd worked a nine-to-five job. His personal office is in our home. When he's home, he's home.

When away, Luis wrote letters to our boys. These writings were treasured words of fatherly counsel as the boys passed from childhood into adulthood. Those letters have provided a lasting heritage. Luis also kept in touch with the children by phone. They could complain and talk to their father, and he would often help settle things between feuding brothers. Sometimes he would say, "We'll talk man-to-man when I get home."

For my part, I dealt with problems on a daily basis, trying not to say, "Wait till your father gets home."

The combination of ministry and travel has had its difficult moments. But when I've been tempted to say I can't handle this, I remind myself that I am willing to work hard for something I really want. The word is not *can't* as much as *won't* in my experience. I have worked hard to make travel my ally, not my enemy.

STRATEGY

An important part of ministry is nurturing your own family physically, emotionally, and spiritually.

For Husbands and Wives

- Build safeguards around the family to keep your marriage strong.
- Establish your family in a stable environment with extended family and church support while Dad is traveling.
- Prayerfully consider lifestyle adjustments that allow your family to be with Dad when he is home and to go with him when travel opportunities arise. One possibility is home-educating the children. A second option is having Dad's office in the home. Third, Mom can be home full-time, or work as a substitute or temporary

employee, so she has the freedom to be home when Dad is home.
- Your children are your God-given priority and should have their needs met. Invest money and time on family fun and trips. Be certain any child care is safe.
- Never tease to hurt another family member.
- Keep the big picture before your eyes. Nothing is more important than leading souls into the eternal kingdom. This ministry is God's call on both your lives. This is also the husband's job and means of providing for his family.

For the Traveler

- Pray continually for your wife, your children, and your work.
- Be at home whenever possible, even for short times between trips.
- Schedule family time.
- Win the hearts of your children by being the father, leader, and educator of the home. Be spiritually strong and sound in doctrine. Remember: You cannot impart to your children what you do not possess yourself.
- Read quality books.
- Avoid entertainment that weakens your spiritual strength.
- Build up the church.
- Use the phone flagrantly to keep in touch with your wife and children. Listen to their complaints. Settle feuds between siblings. Talk "man-to-man" with your sons and heart-to-heart with your daughters.
- Take your wife and children on a ministry trip each year so they know why they sacrifice and can feel a part of the ministry.
- Turn down invitations that cut into family time, and do not indulge in hobbies or interests that take you from the family.
- Invite other travelers to your home. Encourage other men who travel to keep godly priorities.
- If you travel with a large tour, include a pastor in your group. When possible, travel with a partner for accountability.
- Obey God, listen to His voice, do His will, and rest in His perfect timing.

For the Fort Soldier

- Put God first in your life and the rest will fall into place eventually.
- Realize the Lord is your source, strength, and sustainer. Do not ask from your husband what only God can give—understanding. Take your questions and fears to the Lord. Lean on Scripture. God promises never to leave you or forsake you.
- Release your expectations of life and marriage to God and embrace His plans for you.
- Accompany your husband when possible, and be content when you must remain at home.
- Partner with your husband's work through committed prayer. Join with other women to pray for the ministry.
- Your children will mirror your response to Daddy's absence, so set a good example.
- Read to yourself and to your children. Biographies of missionaries (people who did what you are doing now) will encourage, inspire, and give you guidance and empathy.
- Share your children's interests and sports. Have fun together.
- Stop fighting the travel issue; stop counting the time he is away. Make travel your ally, not your enemy.
- Practice grace!

For the Church and Others

- Partner with the family in prayer for their home and their ministry.
- Meet regularly with the wife for prayer and Bible study.
- Establish a flexible accountability group for men, gathering for prayer and Bible study, supporting each other via phone conversations and prayer when each is on the road.
- Send a spiritually uplifting book or tape along on the traveler's next trip.
- Let the family know you care about their difficult times of separation.
- Do fun things together.

Women Who Travel

Ruth the Moabitess said to Naomi, "Let me go to the fields and pick up the leftover grain behind anyone in whose eyes I find favor."

Naomi said to her, "Go ahead, my daughter." So she went out and began to glean in the fields behind the harvesters. As it turned out, she found herself working in a field belonging to Boaz, who was from the clan of Elimelech.

Boaz [said to Ruth], "I've been told all about what you have done for your mother-in-law since the death of your husband—how you left your father and mother and your homeland and came to live with a people you did not know before. May the Lord repay you for what you have done. May you be richly rewarded by the Lord, the God of Israel, under whose wings you have come to take refuge."

So Ruth gleaned in the field until evening. Then she threshed the barley she had gathered, and it amounted to about an ephah. She carried it back to town, and her mother-in-law saw how much she had gathered. Ruth also brought out and gave her what she had left over after she had eaten enough.

—RUTH 2:2–3, 11–12, 17–18

MEME HAD A MILLION THINGS ON HER MIND *as she breezed in the front door, tossed her purse on the couch, and let the dog out the back door. The couple of days immediately preceding a trip were always especially busy for Meme, coordinating arrangements for herself, her son, the dog, the mail, the office staff, and the home.*

She hurried upstairs to change her clothes, passing by her son's empty room. Nicholas had left yesterday to spend some time with his dad.

Suddenly, there was a terrific commotion at the back door. The dog, Christy, was frantic to come inside. "Strange," Meme thought, "I just let her out and she likes being in the backyard."

Meme dashed back downstairs and opened the back door. Christy charged inside and ran frantically through the house, rubbing her face on everything she could reach, including Meme. Christy smelled awful, and within minutes the overwhelming smell of skunk permeated the home and enveloped Meme. She managed to grab Christy and put her back outside. The offensive odor made her eyes water. "I don't have time for this right now," she sighed.

Neither airing out the house nor a shower did much to diminish the horrible smell. The next morning, Meme made a series of phone calls to find someone who would bathe the dog. Dropping Christy off at the groomer's on her way to work, Meme was not only late but well aware she still had an offensive odor about her. But she had to make a presentation before the city manager and his staff before she left for the convention tomorrow.

Sitting in the city hall meeting room, Meme did her best to look composed. Her staff had already razzed her about her new perfume. As the city manager walked into the meeting, his steps faltered. "Something smells like a skunk," he declared.

Meme, looking sheepish, confessed, "It's me."

On her way to the airport the next day, Meme dropped Christy at a friend's house for the ten days she would be away.

"I feel sorry for the person who sits next to you on the plane today," her friend remarked.

"So do I," Meme conceded.

No one said much on the plane, but their wrinkled noses betrayed their annoyance. Once in her hotel room, Meme opened her suitcase and the skunk odor flooded the room. "It wears off," her friend had assured her, but Meme was getting impatient. She grabbed her bottle of expensive perfume and lavishly sprayed it all over her clothes, in the drawers, throughout the closet, and on herself. She did this every day for the entire trip. At first, she smelled like a skunk wearing perfume, but over the course of the week, the perfume became stronger and the skunk odor diminished.

Ironically, this was the trip Meme had extended by a few vacation days in order to attend her sister-in-law's opening night at the theater, visit some relatives, and go to her high school reunion. She looked good, no doubt about that, but she smelled funny.

More and more women find travel part of their lives. How do women fulfill their parenting roles and nurture their marriage while on the road?

TRAVEL AND SINGLE PARENTING
AMELIA SHARP'S STORY

As executive vice-president and CEO of the Convention and Visitors Bureau for a major city, my job involves plenty of night meetings and a fair amount of national and international travel. I am also a single parent to my thirteen-year-old son, Nicholas.

I suffer a lot of guilt, but I need an income. I feel so torn. Basically Nicholas has been bounced from school to day-sitter to night-sitter. I refuse to leave him home alone when I have night meetings, so I arrange for someone to come to the house to "Nic-sit." Business trips have become a little easier as Nicholas gets older. I used to have to pack two suitcases every time I traveled, sending Nicholas off to spend the night somewhere else. Now I have someone stay at the house. But no one can provide the same love and protection as the parent.

Nicholas and I have developed a system of communication for our times apart. My job provides one phone call home each night I am away. In addition, I wear a beeper. If Nicholas sends the numbers 4-1-1 through the beeper, I know he needs some information, but there is no hurry. An 8-1-1 on the beeper indicates it's important for me to call home soon. A 9-1-1 signals an emergency.

Once, at 11:00 A.M., my pager went off during my out-of-town presentation to all the big names. I discreetly turned the pager off, and as I did I saw the 8-1-1. Nicholas was supposed to be at school. I hurried through my presentation and got to a phone.

Nicholas was home, shaky and ill. "Come home right now," he said.

I couldn't go home. I felt helpless. I told him to get some rest, and then I called the overnight sitter.

But even the pager has limits. The hardest times are when I am unreachable because I'm on a plane or outside California. Before a trip, I assemble a detailed itinerary listing who will drop off and pick up Nicholas from school and other activities. The itinerary details both Nicholas's and my schedule, my flights, hotels, and numbers where Nicholas or I can be reached. The list includes phone numbers for the family doctor, available friends, Nicholas's dad, and my office. Medical authority for Nicholas is secured to a trusted friend.

I mail a copy of the itinerary to everyone on the list, and a copy is left with staff at my office. I enclose a note for Nicholas's teacher, alerting her that he may be more sensitive the days I'm away. I make sure the grocery shopping is done and set out extra money for my son's school lunches.

I also installed an alarm system in the house.

For about four days before a trip, Nicholas wants to be with me a lot. He frequently says, "I love you," and tells me he doesn't want me to go. I take him with me as often as possible, and we spend as much time together as we can.

We have a healthy relationship. He's sensitive to my feelings and tries to be protective. I've tried to make him feel secure in our relationship, reminding him I'll always be back. He knows where I am at any given moment, and he knows he can call anytime.

I try to build Nicholas's self-confidence by noting the good character qualities I see in him and the good things he accomplishes. Nicholas wishes his dad and I were still together. This lifestyle has made Nicholas grow up quicker. I thank God for such a capable son.

I bring him a collector pin from each city I visit; Nicholas has quite a collection. I find the pins in airport stores because I don't have time to souvenir shop. This tradition reminds my son that I am thinking of him.

As a single woman, I have two rules for traveling: I never date anyone in the industry, and I never date anyone on the road. I've worked too hard to build a good reputation, and no one is going to destroy it.

I've become very safety-conscious, especially about walking down the street alone at night. Waiting for the airport shuttle to get to my car is the longest part of my trip. I'm so close to home, yet I can't get there any quicker. I just have to wait.

Juggling a more than full-time job, traveling, home maintenance, and parenting Nicholas leaves little time for friends. Yet my friends are my vital support system. I seldom have time to keep in touch, but I want my friends to know I love and appreciate them.

TALK TO YOUR KIDS
NICHOLAS'S STORY

Good-natured thirteen-year-old Nicholas holds down the fort when his mother travels. Here are his observations:

Mom has been traveling intermittently for seven years. Some trips are two weeks; the trip to Japan was one month. When Mom returns from a trip, she has to work longer and harder to catch up at the office, so it seems like she's still gone. I don't get to see her that often.

There are a lot of kids who live with just one of their parents and that parent travels. It's okay. I miss her when she's gone, but I've gotten used to it. She leaves me notes to find and read while she is away. Most of the time, I stay home while Mom is gone.

A couple years she missed my birthday, but it didn't really matter because when she got back she still threw a big party. One time my bunny died while Mom was away and the baby-sitter didn't know what to do. That was hard. It was my Easter bunny.

Mom calls me every day or I call her. Sometimes I forget to tell her something, like that I got an A on my report card, and then I have to wait until the next time she calls. While she's away, I try to work around the house, keep the newspapers picked up, and get the mail. For fun, I build with my Legos and talk on the phone with my friends. Call-waiting is important to Mom and me.

When I'm home alone in the afternoons, I call the police if I hear a strange noise. I can push a button on the house alarm system, and in a few minutes the police will come. The alarm makes me feel safer.

When Mom gets home after a trip, I sometimes give her the cold shoulder. I don't know why I do that or what to do to fix it. I just kinda let it wear off. When she is around, we play board games. Since I love Legos, I build something and share it with her. I go a lot of places with her. I even go to her meetings, though it gets boring sometimes.

For parents who travel, I think it's important to talk to your kid a lot. Ask how they've been doing in school and things like that. See how they are feeling.

WHEN THE WIFE TRAVELS
KIM AND HUGO TEJADA'S STORY

Hugo and Kim Tejada sit on the couch. When his arm is not around her shoulders, his hand is holding hers. In their thirties, they are just beginning their second year of marriage.

Kim's travel is part of her work as an auditor for the Federal Government. "When I took the job, I was told there would be 25 percent travel," she said. "It turned into 50 percent, and now it's about 33 percent. When I was single, I was looking forward to traveling throughout the United States. But I became more and more uncomfortable with being alone in a hotel at night."

Hugo, who is employed in the hospitality industry, worries about his wife. "I hate having her stay in a hotel. It's a dangerous place. So many of those room keys are floating around because people take the keys with them." Hugo recommends travelers stay at hotels where codes on computerized room keys are changed after each visitor.

Kim dispelled the glamorous travel myth. "There is not a trip where something at the hotel does not go wrong," she said, "like the key not working, the tub backing up, waiting three hours for an iron, arriving and finding no reservation—and by the time I figure out how to work the thermostat, it's time to go home. One time I was on the twelfth floor and had to walk down all the stairs at 4:00 A.M. due to a false fire alarm. Another trip, I stayed in a gigantic hotel where people were partying above me. I've learned to ask for no smoking rooms."

The unpredictability of the travel schedule is another source of frustration. "Things change hourly," Kim said. "The worst was last summer. We'd been married three months, and I had to go to Oregon from mid-July to the end of October. I feel guilty each time I have to go."

Hugo smiled. "She gets this look and says, 'Oh, ummm,' and I say, 'Where are you going?' "

Kim noted, "I try not to leave my packing to the night before I leave because that's our last night together. I'm a professional packer. Everything is condensed and lightweight. My cosmetic bag is always ready, and I've learned to take personal reading material with me for those times when I'm stuck in an airport or on the plane."

To nurture their marriage while Kim is away, the Tejadas talk each night by phone. "I'm a wimp and a crybaby about being away," she admitted. "Hugo encourages me, reminding me it's only a few more days and I need to do my job. He's a real motivator."

Kim looks forward to the evening phone calls but tries not to think about Hugo during the day. "It makes me miss him more," she said. "But missing Hugo reminds me to pray for him."

Hugo takes the initiative in keeping their relationship strong. Sometimes he flies to see her on the weekends, and he sends cards. On the day Kim returns from a trip, Hugo cleans the house and greets his wife with fresh flowers.

Maintaining spiritual disciplines is a challenge for Kim when she travels. "Sometimes it is harder to have a quiet time each day when I'm away because I have a much more relaxed schedule," she related. "Since I don't have to commute or fix meals, there is not as much regimen in my day. At home, I use my commute for my quiet time. When I'm away, I read my Bible in the evening, but missing Hugo becomes a distraction."

Hugo purposely concentrates on his spiritual life to help him get through their separation. "I use the time to get together with the guys for Bible study and fellowship, for my accountability, to seek God, to draw close to Him, to remember I'm a Christian and what all that means," he said. "It's important for me to meet with the guys to keep my focus on the Lord, and that's good for our marriage. In praying without ceasing, my thought life becomes a conversation with God. I read my Bible for half an hour before work each day."

Kim concluded, "I don't like the travel now that I'm married. Not being with Hugo on a daily basis is the hardest part. It's a job until we start our family, and then I will quit. What makes the travel endurable is knowing I won't be doing this for the rest of my life."

EPILOGUE

Kim traded business travel for full-time mothering when she and Hugo welcomed the arrival of their baby daughter, Moriah.

STRATEGY

Nurturing a marriage relationship, mothering children, and making a home while traveling for business is an especially demanding lifestyle. This challenging situation requires forethought and planning.

For Husbands and Wives

- Communicate by phone; carry a beeper. Let your family know they can call you anytime.
- Get call-waiting phone service so you don't miss opportunities to talk.
- Ask your spouse and children about their day.
- Celebrate special days such as birthdays, even if you have to wait until Mom returns from a trip.
- Children should not be left alone. Make arrangements for child care at all hours.
- Notice your children's good character qualities and praise their efforts.

For the Traveler

- Women commonly report they feel guilt over being away from their children and husband. Be together as much as possible when you are home.

- Reassure your children that you will be back. Help them feel secure in your relationship with them and your love for them.
- Take the family on trips when possible.
- Occasionally children can accompany you to the office and to meetings to get a flavor for what you do.
- Have family traditions such as bringing home a souvenir pin from each city you visit.
- Prior to a trip, assemble a detailed itinerary including contact names and phone numbers. Give a copy of the itinerary to each of your support people.
- Systematize your packing. Pack early so you can enjoy the evening with your loved ones prior to your departure. Take a good book on your trip.
- When you travel, take precautions to stay safe. Stay at hotels that change computerized room keys for each guest.
- For single women, don't date within the industry or on the road. You are on company time. Don't risk your reputation, integrity, or job. Likewise, it is inappropriate for a married woman to go to dinner with a man other than her husband. Ask a third party to come along.
- Remain consistent in your personal devotions.

For the Fort Soldier

- Encourage your wife. She feels emotionally torn between her desire to be with her family and the job she needs to do.
- Call often. Send cards and flowers.
- Visit her if she is on an extended trip.
- Be especially attentive to your children and have fun with them.
- Use your time wisely.
- Keep the home tidy and the laundry done. Your wife should not have to return to a disaster.

For the Church and Others

- Help transport children to school and activities.
- Care for children when you can.

- Offer to be an emergency contact the school can call if necessary.
- Pet sit.
- If you live close-by, keep an eye on the family's house while they are away.

CHAPTER NINE

Traveling With Members of the Opposite Sex

Test everything. Hold on to the good. Avoid every kind of evil.

—1 *Thessalonians* 5:21–22

L OGIC SAYS THAT IF I AM *also following the biblical injunction to abstain from even the appearance of evil (1 Thessalonians 5:22), I will also abstain from the evil itself. My philosophy is that if you take care of how things look, you take care of how things are."*

—Jerry Jenkins
(from his book *Hedges: Loving Your Marriage Enough to Protect It*)

———

In today's workplace men and women often find themselves working closely with the opposite sex. Workers must employ a strong, uncompromising set of boundaries and precautions to protect and preserve their marriages.

MAINTAINING CONSISTENT STANDARDS
JEANNE STERN'S STORY

My job as vice-president of sales requires day and overnight trips a couple of times a month. Sometimes these trips must be made with a male co-worker. Due to the nature of my job, chances for interaction

103

with men are probably greater than most, but the standards I live by at work remain the same in every area of my life.

I maintain a professional set of boundaries and precautions consistent with who I am in all situations in life, whether at work, shopping, at church, mixing with friends, or in my personal time.

Certain situations at work, such as cold calling, meetings with clients, and training employees, naturally have a larger potential for contact with members of the opposite sex. There is a respect I must have for myself. I don't let anyone dictate a situation with me. I am there for a purpose, and I don't get into inappropriate conversation or jesting. I keep my conversation mainstream and work oriented. I do not talk about my personal life or make suggestive overtones.

Sometimes an innocent offer such as, "Can I get you something? Would you like a cup of coffee?" can be perceived the wrong way. I ignore any inappropriate remarks that are made.

Physically, it is important to maintain my personal space and not lean over or touch other people, especially men. I limit body contact to a short, professional handshake, and I am careful with the type of eye contact I make. I dress and conduct myself modestly.

Making conversation is the hardest part of a trip with male coworkers. If I know and am comfortable with the person I am traveling with, there is no need to talk. I can be quiet or read.

While out of town, I stay in hotels with groups of sales people. I get my own door and avoid lunches alone with another man by taking a third party along. Evening entertainment is not an option for me.

There is plenty of gossip in the industry linking people's names together. There is still a double standard for men and women. When employees act inappropriately, it adversely affects everyone in the business. Company morale declines, business declines, marriages suffer, harassment charges are filed, and people lose their jobs.

My husband, Shawn, has concerns about the company's responsibility for his wife's safety. I am continually alert to the environment. There are people at work I know I need to be on my guard with all the time.

When I'm away on a trip, I have complete confidence in Shawn to take care of our home and our two daughters. Before I leave, I prepare meals and clothes for the family at home. I leave notes and presents for my husband and children while I am away to make the time special. I call home to keep in touch.

I help carry the financial responsibility of the family. Being a working mother has affected my children. My youngest daughter suffered a broken leg while at a baby-sitter's. I experience a lot of guilt, especially when I forget something I promised my daughter and then remember the promise when I am out of town.

As a working woman, I must do double duty. On a daily basis I care for the physical needs of my home and family. I get up early to complete the cooking and cleaning. When I am traveling for work, I can't neglect the things of the home or there won't be a home. My job is to work smarter, not later. I don't leave my family for unimportant stuff like going up the night before a business trip. I negotiated to work through the lunch break so I can leave work an hour earlier each day. I get the job done, but it's never been my goal to be a cookie-cutter person.

Scripturally, my strength comes from the "do unto others" verses in the Bible. These motivate and inspire me. Matthew 25:40 tells us, "I tell you the truth, whatever you did for one of the least of these brothers of mine, you did for me." People are people, friends are friends—no matter where you find them. I don't differentiate between whether a relationship is from work, church, or the neighborhood. I enjoy my work, and I enjoy people.

LOVE THAT GOES BEYOND THE PHYSICAL
BY TERRY SCOTT

As a commercial airline pilot, my husband travels throughout the country and abroad with men and women. He is exposed to many situations where temptations can be a real threat.

Jeff and I married after a whirlwind courtship, and much of our attraction for each other was based on physical appearances. We are now a family of seven with two dogs and a tankful of fish. Struggling with my weight has been a source of conflict between Jeff and me; caring for my physical appearance has always taken a backseat to everyone else's needs.

Our third child has severe asthma, eczema, and allergies. Learning to care for him has seemed the equivalent of earning a medical degree. Sometimes I wish I were the spouse with the career of traveling, hotels, restaurants, and adult conversation.

During the time my husband spends away from home, his thoughts, concerns, actions, and conversations usually revolve around us. He is known as a family man. We have established boundaries for protecting our marriage because Jeff and I are committed to keeping our spouse and the family first.

My husband's extra time away from home is spent doing things to make life easier for me. He plans for Christmas, picks up birthday gifts, corresponds with friends and relatives; and does the clothes shopping. Jeff plans our annual vacations. With a large family, there is not enough time for me to read the newspaper. My husband saves interesting news clippings to share with us when he returns.

During the years of child-rearing, Jeff and I have both gladly put aside activities and friendships that would exclude our family. There are no hunting, fishing, golfing, racquetball, or ski trips without including the family. For us, Sunday worship has never been optional, but extra activities are carefully selected, making sure we maintain plenty of family time.

We all agree that the best way to maintain a healthy home is to communicate! Every day that Jeff travels he calls home at least once. The children line up to have their turn to talk to Dad. Jeff may hear the same news from each of us, but you would never know by his response. Another way we help keep Dad current on our lives is by writing him letters. The letters are not mailed, but are hand delivered to Jeff when he returns home.

Christ is the center of our individual lives, marriage, and growing family. God has promised to be with us always, even in our temptations and errors, growing our marriage relationship in spite of this earthly conflict with weight. "Trust in the Lord with all your heart and lean not on your own understanding; in all your ways acknowledge him and he will make your paths straight" (Prov. 3:5–6).

YOUR MOST IMPORTANT RELATIONSHIP
JOHN BENTLEY'S STORY

As the owner of my own company, I don't want business travel to strain the marriages of any of the people who work for me. I don't want anyone to experience the pain of divorce. My best witness is to the people close to me, then to the people I work with, and then to the people in the world.

Toward that end, the company has implemented a proactive approach to support families. When a prospective employee is being interviewed, their spouse is brought in during the interview process. I sit the wife (or husband) down and give them the worst-case travel scenario. Then I ask if the spouse can handle it, because if they are not sure, now is the time to speak up. I assure the couple that our office is available if help is needed at home while an employee is on the road. I offer a $100 bonus for each time a couple goes to counseling if they are having marriage problems.

Frequently I give the staff books that help build their marriage relationships. We are very liberal about getting information that is good for the body of the company as well as good for the body of Christ. The company subscribes to helpful publications like Larry Burkett's *Money Matters* newsletter. These materials are available in the lunchroom. I impress debt-free living on everyone, providing a livable salary plus commissions. By living on their draw, they can use the commissions to pay down debt or as cash for larger needs.

Each year the company tithes to a variety of places. Staff members make recommendations ranging from community library projects and reading-to-the-blind programs to broader Christian organizations. The company sponsors missions trips for those in our office who want to go. At the Christmas party we review where the money went over the year.

We strive for a team spirit in the company. Our office maintains regular travel schedules so families can plan around trips. When someone is out, the rest of us cover for them. In the office, we all handle "customers," not "territories."

The most important relationship, besides your relationship with Christ, is the relationship with your spouse. I encourage staff members to take their spouses on trips whenever they can. The company pays for their lodging and gas. Male and female employees who are not married to each other never travel alone together.

STRATEGY

While traveling with members of the opposite sex provides added opportunity for temptation, diligence can assure your "marriage [is] honored by all, and the marriage bed kept pure" (Heb. 13:4).

For Husbands and Wives

- Abstain from even the appearance of evil. If you take care of how things look, you take care of how things are.
- Employ a strong, uncompromising set of boundaries and precautions to protect your marriage.
- Set aside activities and friendships that exclude family.
- Carefully select activities and church programs that enhance but don't overburden the family.
- Discover and nurture the special talents and characteristics of each family member.

For the Traveler

- Dress and move modestly. Maintain an appropriate physical space. Body contact with anyone other than your spouse should be limited to a professional, brief handshake. Don't let your eyes linger.
- Respect yourself. Don't allow anyone to dictate a situation for you. Be aware of your environment. Avoid people who make you feel uncomfortable.
- Keep conversations work related. Don't talk about your personal

life. Never make suggestive overtones. Keep all compliments professional, not focused on another's appearance.

- Ignore any off-color comments.
- Don't force conversation. Take along a book to occupy travel time.
- Remember, any inappropriate behavior destroys your integrity, reputation, family relationships, business, and company morale.
- Don't be away from home longer than is completely necessary.
- Whenever possible, stay in hotels with groups of people. Don't go out to eat alone with someone of the opposite sex. Take along a third party at least, or better yet, go in a group.
- Refrain from any evening entertainment that has even "the appearance of evil."
- Communicate openly with your family and your boss concerning your travel activities.
- Reassure your spouse of his/her attractiveness to you and of your continuing faithfulness.
- Use free time when away to shop for family needs and gifts. Help plan vacations and holidays.

For the Fort Soldier

- Your good care of the children and home while your spouse is away provides special comfort and security for your mate. Knowing the children are well allows the traveler to focus completely on the business to be done.
- Give the children time on the phone with the traveling parent.
- Encourage the children to write letters to the traveling spouse. Even if the letters are not received and read until the traveler returns, the news and thoughts inside are still important for keeping communication open.

For the Church and Others

- Be careful not to gossip or link people's names together.
- Do not send male and female co-workers or church representatives on trips together.
- Allow families to choose what activities and programs to participate in that best suit their family and lifestyle.

Workaholics

Do not wear yourself out to get rich; have the wisdom to show restraint. Cast but a glance at riches, and they are gone, for they will surely sprout wings and fly off to the sky like an eagle.

"Do not store up for yourselves treasures on earth, where moth and rust destroy, and where thieves break in and steal. But store up for yourselves treasures in heaven, where moth and rust do not destroy, and where thieves do not break in and steal. For where your treasure is, there your heart will be also."

—*Proverbs 23:4–5; Matthew 6:19–21*

T WO NURSES SAT ON THE BALCONY *watching their children play on the private beach. Each year the physician they worked with invited his staff and their families to his lake cottage for a summer picnic and swim.*

The newest staff member surveyed the peaceful scene. "It must be nice," she said. "Obviously being a doctor pays well."

The physician's wife appeared with a tray of cold drinks and snacks in time to overhear her guest's comments.

"It probably seems extravagant to some," she smiled. "But this cottage has saved our family. We bought this place eighteen years ago when the twins were babies. This is the only place we are a family, where the children have uninterrupted dinners with their dad. When we're at the house in town, my husband gets phone calls around the clock. Even when he's not on call and on his days off, he winds up on the phone all day, working. But no one can reach him here at the lake. He can go outside and play with the children. In the city their dad is a doctor. But at the lake, he is their dad."

Workaholics may not be out of town, but they are frequently not at home. Some people are driven internally to work longer and harder. Some are driven externally onto the fast-paced treadmill by their jobs, residency programs, internships, or graduate studies.

Prayer Is the Key
Kristin and Barry Ford's Story

As vice-president of a family-owned moving agency, my husband, Barry, works a minimum of sixty hours each week. Though he doesn't leave the house until 8:30 A.M., he begins his work on the home computer at 5:30 A.M. He works Saturdays until 4:00 P.M. and frequently works on Sunday.

Married for eleven years, we have functioned this way for nine. Our oldest daughter is in elementary school, and we have two pre-schoolers.

Barry works with his father, brother, and three partners. Like his father, who built the business, Barry keeps long hours and falls asleep as soon as he comes home at night. The responsibilities of running the home and caring for the children fall almost entirely to me.

We both fall into bed exhausted each night. I'm concerned for Barry; he runs on the work treadmill like a mouse on a wheel. He's so tired. My dad worked just like that, and he had his first heart attack at age forty-seven.

The year I was home with three preschoolers (Neesha was three years old, Mason was two, and Breanna was a baby) was the worst year of our marriage. Barry was working eighteen-hour days and often staying the night at the job site. I would go three days without seeing him, and because of the nature of the moving business, most of the jobs fell on a Friday through Sunday—our weekends. Since she didn't know him, Breanna wouldn't go to Barry until she was almost three years old.

I developed my own little world aside from Barry. I took the children to church by myself, had my own set of friends, followed my own schedule, and developed my own interests. Barry just worked.

One day I found an old skeleton key, and the Lord used it to remind me that prayer is the key to handling life with a workaholic. I began spending purposeful time in prayer. I began praying for Barry, for the children, and for our relationships as a family. I trusted the Lord to maximize my limited spiritual training with the children, to keep them close to Him.

As a result, I'm doing better at accepting Barry for who he is. I think even if he worked for someone he would still work too many hours. I have stopped putting friends in the place of my husband because Barry should be my best friend. Now I ask Barry about going places together, whether it's to the park with the children or to attend a concert with another couple. I enjoy being with him. Barry is easy to talk with, and he gives great advice. He frequently tells me he loves me and compliments me on how I look. Neither of us grew up in affectionate homes, so we are learning together how to be affectionate with each other.

This past year has been the best year of our marriage. I've come to rely on God's faithfulness. Barry and I are communicating more, and we've taken vacations together. While Barry is working at home in the early mornings, he oversees the children while I slip off to the gym. We make a point of trying to have breakfast together as a family in the midst of getting Neesha ready for school and Barry off to work.

I use the phone regularly to find out when Barry thinks he'll be home in the evenings. I've learned to encourage Barry to come home well before the children's bedtime or wait until 9:00 P.M., after we have done our bedtime routine of prayer and Scripture memory and they are tucked in. Otherwise, the children are so excited to see him that they stay up late, and they are tired and grumpy for school the next morning. It throws our whole day off.

The children and I have our dinner together, then I spend personal time with them, tuck them into bed, and have dinner waiting for Barry when he comes in. I sit with Barry while he eats; that has become our time to talk. If I need to go somewhere in the evening, I let Barry know ahead of time and he tries to bring work home so he can be with the children.

Although my husband works lots of hours, there are some blessings to owning our own business. Working with his dad has enabled Barry to develop the father-son relationship. Barry's dad now regrets not spending time with his three sons when they were young because he was so busy working.

Involvement with Promise Keepers has influenced Barry to spend more time with his children, talking and playing with them on their level. Barry disciplines less and plays more with our son, Mason. The two of them are like a couple of kids together.

Barry meets with three other men in our church one day each week for an early morning accountability group. They ask each other how their relationship is with the Lord, their wife, their children, and their work. They pray for one another.

Yes, I see improvements. The key for me has been prayer.

STAYING ON HIS SIDE
BY GWEN DAILEY

When we married, I was in nursing school and Pete was a laboratory technologist working in a medical lab. After we had been married three years, Pete decided to go to graduate school. By then I had worked as a nurse for a year, and we both felt ready to start our family. We moved from Southern California to Berkeley, where Pete began graduate work and a half-time job, while I became a full-time homemaker and a mother-to-be.

For eight years Pete would be gone all day, come home for dinner, then return to work in the evening. He worked all day Saturday and often Saturday evening. Sunday we went to church in the morning, and Pete napped in the afternoon. He needed the rest, but I wanted some company, and I wanted Pete to spend time with our two children.

Normal activities of daily living became big, tiring productions. It was tough having to do all the grocery shopping and necessary errands with the children. I never knew if I could find someone I trusted to watch them while I got my hair cut, visited the dentist, or saw the doctor. Have you ever installed new seat belts in a twenty-five-year-old car—which means crawling underneath—while keeping an eye on a five-year-old and a two-year-old? Well, I did, because I knew that if I didn't, it wouldn't get done.

Being on my own so much of the time forced me to become more responsible and self-reliant. I learned to "slug" through a project, even when I didn't feel like it. I learned to depend on God even when the emotion was not there. I found creative ways to increase our time together. I try to get all the everyday work—laundry and house cleaning—out of the way, so when we do have time together I am not too busy to pay attention to Pete.

I have learned it's okay to take care of myself and get a break. At various times I have hired a mother's helper (a friend's daughter) to help with housework or watch the children while I did a special project. I might also exchange baby-sitting with a trusted friend. Sometimes I would get up early, before Pete left for school, to go jogging or swimming. Just having that time out of the apartment and alone with my thoughts really refreshed me. It was a great time for prayer too.

Making sure I got enough rest and a nap every day were important. As my children grew too old to nap, I trained them to spend some quiet time on their beds in the afternoon. They could look at books and play with quiet toys while I rested.

The best way I learned to take care of myself was to watch my attitude. I regret that as the years went by, with no end to the stressful schedule in sight, I became discontented. I compared myself with others, and when someone took pity on me or said, "You deserve better than that," I felt even more depressed.

But the Lord has been teaching me the biblical principle of Philippians 4:11: "I have learned to be content whatever the circumstances." Discontentment comes from not trusting God enough with my circumstances. It helped to change my expectations. There is no constitutional right to working only forty hours per week. We don't have to be like everyone else, even when there is pressure to conform.

I learned to speak positively and respectfully about Pete to the children, reinforcing Pete's leadership in the home while he was gone. Finally, I learned to see things from Pete's perspective. I would tell myself, "Here he is, doing his best to support his family by working, and you are unhappy. If he didn't work, you would be even more unhappy." First Timothy 5:8 says, "If anyone does not provide for his relatives, and especially for his immediate family, he has denied the faith and is worse than an unbeliever." It was vital that I stay on Pete's side.

FOLLOWING MY HUSBAND AROUND THE WORLD
GRACE AND PAT CHURCH'S STORY

I often ask Pat why he is so driven. During our twenty-three years of marriage, my husband has worked hard and had extremely limited time with the family. His job with a major bank has included eleven moves in fourteen years, ten of them overseas with frequent business travel. In retrospect, Pat's demanding schedule has been difficult for me, but something I've had to just keep working at.

Moving is like transplanting a plant. Initially the plant dies, and then it grows again. The dying part is hard. Living overseas was something I wanted to do, but it was also challenging. It took six months to adjust to each new place. Pat would go to work where there was a degree of familiarity for him, but I had to find my own way around. With every new place I had to find a new doctor, new dentist, new stores, reliable household help, schools for the children, and hopefully, new friends.

Once we had to live for six months without our belongings. It was a real eye-opener to see how well we managed, and how much more time I had with less things to take care of!

As far as parenting, I did everything. I was home, so I was involved with our sons' school activities. I did all their spiritual training. I was lonely for Pat, and I wanted him to be involved with the family. When I told him how I felt, he would tell me how to be, and that was very frustrating.

I saw other women drink to compensate for their loneliness overseas. Alcohol was served at every social event. Some wives had affairs. Their commitment to their marriage was not strong enough. Couples must be committed to each other and to the marriage, no matter where they live, if they are going to make it.

I began a little exercise book in which I recorded prayer requests, answers to prayer, and special verses I liked to memorize. Two of my favorite Scriptures were Psalm 27:14, "Wait for the Lord; be strong and take heart and wait for the Lord," and Philippians 4:13, "I can do everything through him who gives me strength."

I have learned that my head has to rule my heart. I have to do what I have to do. Correct communication between a husband and wife helps, and Pat and I didn't always have that.

It was important for me to make each place a home for my family. As the wife, I have to give more because there are so many demands on my husband and his time. Whether one spouse "gives" more than the other cannot be an issue; being committed to one another and our marriage is what is important.

Now one of the things Pat and I do for our marriage is to spend as many weekends as we can camping at a lake in the Sierras. Praise God for the gift of the lake. There are no phones, no demands, and no computers—just nature and the campfire.

If I could do it all again I'd do a better job. I'd be more understanding with the children. As hard as it is, the wife must be supportive of her husband. Going overseas has been an adventure. I'd do it again in a minute. I enjoyed seeing other countries, experiencing their cultures and their foods. There are plusses and minuses to everything, but the negatives recede in light of the positives of accompanying my husband around the world.

STRATEGY

Here are some strategies families of workaholics have used to survive their stressful lifestyle.

For Husbands and Wives

- Establish a place to get away from work. If finances allow, buy a cottage by the lake or a cabin in the mountains.
- Schedule a family outing each Saturday or take a drive after church on Sunday. Get away from the phone and the pull of work. Jealously guard the day you have together.
- Unplug the phone during meals and family devotions.
- Find a meal time you can share as a family. If not dinner, then breakfast or lunch.
- Do family devotions at this time as well. Read a portion of Scripture aloud, practice a verse you are memorizing together, sing a song, and pray. Devotions do not have to be long, especially when little children are involved.

For the Workaholic

- Protect family time by conducting business during business hours. Work smart. Get the job done during the work day.
- Call home daily just to say "I love you."
- Even if you have only a short time between appointments, it is worth it to stop in at home.
- Work through frustrations and difficult situations with your wife. Be there for her when she needs you.
- Take leadership of your children's spiritual training.
- Make an effort to be involved with your family. Invest time in your children, play with the children. The best prevention for peer pressure is a strong relationship with Dad.
- Make family vacations a priority—don't wait until you "have time."
- Schedule an accountability group once a week with men you respect. Ask each other these questions: How is your relationship with the Lord? How is your relationship with your wife? How is your relationship with your children? How are things at your work? How can I pray for you?

For the Fort Soldier

- Remember, prayer is the key. Talk to God about your situation.
- Practice contentment with how things are. Release expectations of how things "should be." Be accepting and flexible as opposed to resentful.
- Accept your husband for who he is.
- Commit yourself 100 percent to your marriage.
- Do not fall into the trap of living separate lives.
- Seek your husband's counsel first on decisions and concerns. Set aside time to talk with him when he comes home.
- Maintain a positive and respectful attitude toward your husband when talking with the children.
- Try to see things from your husband's perspective. Stay on his side.
- Take care of yourself, get a break. If Dad is not available to take over with the children for a while, hire a mother's helper (a friend's daughter) to help with housework or to play with the children while you do a special project or get a nap.
- Teach the children to have a quiet time of looking at books or playing with quiet toys on their bed while you take a short nap to recharge.
- If relocating would give you more time with your husband, move.
- Sometimes you will need to just "slug" though tough situations when you are already tired and emotionally depleted.
- Don't drown your loneliness in alcohol or other addictive and destructive behaviors.
- Attend a women's Bible study (such as Joy of Living, Bible Study Fellowship, or Precepts) that provides a children's program.
- Journal your prayers and record helpful Scriptures, as well as prayer requests and their answers.

For the Church and Others

- Be that trustworthy person your friend calls to care for her children when a need arises.
- Trade child care.

- Visit.
- Encourage the family to participate in church activities and Bible studies. If there is not a Bible study in progress, start one, even if it is only with one other person.

When Money Is the Bottom Line

If anyone does not provide for his relatives, and especially
for his immediate family, he has denied the faith
and is worse than an unbeliever.

—1 TIMOTHY 5:8

J O'S ADOLESCENT SON, AARON, WAS TESTING *the boundaries again. Having grown taller than his mother, Aaron periodically ignored her instructions and challenged her authority. Jo's husband, Ray, began driving a truck the day after their wedding. His trips brought him home one or two weekends each month. Their relationship was maintained through nightly phone calls, and Jo didn't want each conversation to center around discipline. Juggling part-time nursing with full-time single parenting three children was overwhelming.*

Mulling over her frustrations at church that morning, Jo mused, "I'm in this unique situation. I'm married but single."

"Perhaps Aaron is trying to find his identity as a young man," sympathized a friend. "To help him feel he has a clear role in the family, you could give Aaron some of the male-oriented jobs around the house," he suggested, "such as mowing the lawn, changing the furnace filters, tuning the car, fixing the plumbing, and taking out the trash."

"For as long as we've been married, Ray has come home long enough to get a nap, get his clothes laundered and packed back into the truck. Ray's clothes do not hang in our bedroom closet, they hang in his truck," Jo explained. "I mow the lawn, change the furnace filters, tune the car, fix the plumbing, and take out the trash. Aaron has always seen his mother do

these jobs. At our house there are no 'male' jobs because the children and I either do it ourselves or pay to have it done. It doesn't matter if it is a man's job or a woman's job, we are all pulling together."

Jo almost laughed at the surprised look on her friend's face. He only wanted to help but honestly had no idea of the unique challenges facing a family with a full-time traveling dad.

"I guess I'll have to give the problem some more thought," he mumbled. "And I'll pray about it."

"Me too," Jo smiled. "Me too."

Sometimes the best way to financially support the family is through a job that dictates travel. For pilots and truck drivers, for instance, travel is the job. What happens when circumstances box a family into the travel lifestyle?

"DADDY DRIVES AN EIGHTEEN-WHEELER"
MICHELLE AND DEWAYNE BYFORD'S STORY

Like my father, my husband, Dewayne, drives a truck for a living. As an only child, I remember Dad would leave on Sunday and return on Friday. Dewayne's schedule is the same. Occasionally he may be gone two weeks, should his route take him to one of the farthest of the forty-eight states or Canada.

Realistically, Dewayne can't do anything else. In our small town in Arkansas, there are no other jobs to support our family with three children, a car payment, and a house payment. Dewayne's education is another factor. He passed his GED after we were married. Though he has felt convicted about being home more, he is not qualified to do anything else. Financially, his profession allows me to be home with our three boys.

In 1994 Dewayne came off the road to work at a local boating business. We thought having him home would be our dream come true. But his salary was only half what driving the truck provided, so Dewayne ended up being away from home even more working overtime or side jobs. Saturdays were the worst for me. Previously the children and I had all-day Saturday with Dewayne, but in the boating business, weekends and holidays are necessary workdays. I hated it. Not only was Dewayne away from the family more than when he was on the truck, we were not making financial ends meet. We didn't starve, but I couldn't buy the children shoes, either. Worry over the finances made Dewayne critical.

My husband went back to driving truck and our family returned to our familiar pattern. My days are filled with caring for our sons, church and school activities, piano lessons, and scout meetings. Two days a week I clean our church.

During spring break and each summer, the boys and I pile in the truck and go on a trip with Dewayne. It's nice to be together and show the children some of the wonders of our country like Mt. Shasta and Donner Lake in California, Hoover Dam in Nevada, and watch them pick up salt off the great salt flats in Utah. We've visited Indian reservations in New Mexico and watched huge ships sailing the Pacific Ocean. These trips give the children and me firsthand experience with Dewayne's life on the road. Because Dewayne is accustomed to driving alone, he's not much of a talker on our trips together, so I take some good books along.

Our three boys don't get upset when Dewayne leaves. They don't really know any other lifestyle. They know what Daddy does and why.

My most painful struggle occurred in July 1991 when both my parents were hospitalized in two separate facilities 430 miles from my home. My two small sons and I stayed in a motel near the hospitals, in a town I knew nothing about, until my parents were well enough to be released. I wanted Dewayne to be with me, but he said, "Honey, I have to go back to work because right now I'm the only one in the family who is working." Without anyone to talk to, and without Jesus in my life for comfort, the pain and anxiety was unbearable. That was when I realized I needed God in my life.

I have plenty of difficult days when Dewayne is away, days when something breaks down or when the children are more than I can handle alone. Pretty typical problems, actually. My support system while Dewayne is on the truck is my pastor's wife and the youth director's wife. They listen when I need to talk and talk when I need to listen.

Sustaining my marriage takes more work. It's hard to communicate with someone who is not there. Dewayne and I talk on the phone often, but it's just not the same. I feel serious discussions should wait until we're together, so I keep things to myself longer than I would like. I don't like to worry my husband. I lean on the Lord to be my strength and sufficiency.

Dewayne utilizes Christian radio and cassette tapes to keep in touch with godly principles, as he has no other support on the road. When Dewayne is surrounded by ungodly influences, he is strengthened by Psalm 119:11, "I have hidden your word in my heart that I might not sin against you."

To allow Dewayne time with the boys and me rather than fixing the sink and mowing the lawn, I don't let minor repairs and chores build up for my husband to come home to. If I can do it, I do it. If I cannot do a repair but money is available to have someone else come in and do it, I make those arrangements.

For a while Dewayne spent every weekend repairing his old pickup truck. He finally purchased a truck that would not require all his time, and the payment was no more than what he was spending to keep the old one running. We arranged for me to have power of attorney so I could sign necessary papers without Dewayne having to take time off from work.

When my day throws me an unexpected curve, I lean on Matthew 6:25, "Therefore I tell you, do not worry about your life, what you will eat or drink; or about your body, what you will wear. Is not life more important than food, and the body more important than clothes?" Verse 34 continues, "Therefore do not worry about tomorrow, for tomorrow will worry about itself. Each day has enough trouble of its own."

FROM BITTER TO BETTER
LISA AND BRAD GILL'S STORY

My husband, Brad, and I both come from broken families with undependable fathers, so we have determined to do better for our own children.

Though it is a dangerous job, when Brad had the chance to become a Deputy Marshall, we felt it would be a good career and financial move for our family.

Brad has traveled since we were married. In the Coast Guard he would ship out for a month and a half, then be home for a month. Assigned to Treasure Island in the San Francisco Bay, Brad wore a pager so the boat could summon him at any hour. We had to take two cars wherever we went in case he was called to the boat, and he had to remain within a certain radius of the boat at all times. I wanted to throw that pager away.

Presently, Brad commutes two-and-a-half hours, works long days, and is sent away for extended periods of time. He was away three months for training, then sent out immediately for another month. The boys and I stayed with friends until I could move us into our own home. I was trying to set up housekeeping in a new place, the children had chicken pox, and the car broke down. We were freezing in Vallejo, California, while Brad was sitting in a luxury hotel in 80° Hawaii.

A chief's wife once told me, "This lifestyle will either make you bitter or better." I was more on the bitter side the first years of our marriage. But it was wasted energy on my part.

The hardest thing for me is coping with behavior problems and being consistent with our three boys. A strong-willed child can really wear a parent out. When Brad is away, the boys cling to me. Their attitudes change, and when I ask what's wrong they tell me they miss Dad. It almost did me in when one son reversed his toilet training for the three months Brad was away.

I keep Brad posted on what I observe in the boys. Over the phone I try not to cross that fine line between telling Brad all the negative things and letting him know what's going on at home. Carrying the responsibility for the family and our protection while not being here physically is the hardest aspect for Brad.

Rather than tear Brad down to the children, I call a friend when I'm angry and need to talk to someone. I don't want to be the one who holds him back. It all boils down to contentment. Even though this is not the life I would have chosen, God knows what is best.

When Brad is away, I read the Psalms. I find myself saying, "Yeah, David. I understand." Writing every night during those long trips is therapy for me and gives a continuity to what's going on day to day. Wherever he goes, Brad keeps up daily Bible reading and attends church services. Our relationship with the Lord has helped our marriage and family to survive.

Each time we are reassigned, it takes about six months for me to stop feeling lonely at the new location. I can't lollygag around for months at a time looking for a church. I need a supportive church right away, hopefully with people who have things in common with me.

It's a great encouragement when a friend calls to say she is praying for me, brings a meal for the boys and me, invites us over without waiting for Brad to be around, or offers to have the children play at her home so I can run errands. I'm careful not to overbook my time, and Brad encourages me to have a steady baby-sitter for the children once a week so I can attend Bible study. Brad and I have a date night once a week when he's in town; it's important to know I'm still his best friend.

Today, if Brad came home and said he was going to be gone for a month, I could handle it. Life goes on.

IF I CAN DO THIS, ANYONE CAN
MICHELLE AND SCOTT LAURANCE'S STORY

For many years my husband, Scott, dreamed of becoming a sales representative for a manufacturing company. When he got the job, we knew it was his chance financially. No other job offers this kind of income based on experience, without a college education.

Scott's territory includes the western United States. During his first year on the road, he called home each night, and I'd cry and tell him all that went wrong that day. "What do you want me to do about it a thousand miles away?" Scott would say. That hurt my feelings, but it also made me stronger.

If I can handle this lifestyle, anyone can. My personality is highly emotional. By nature I'm a worrywart, not easygoing. Through Scott's travel, I've learned to be easier on myself. The evenings when I'm so exhausted I can't think about making dinner, I'll order pizza and not feel guilty about it. The boys and I get to bed by 9:00 P.M., 8:00 if we're really tired. If the children seem extra stressed on a certain day, I put them to bed earlier and let them read for an hour. I can turn off the television or turn down the music. I control the peace in the home.

I've learned to like myself, to enjoy my time when Scott's away, to put my energy into other things. As the boys get older, I have more time to get to know myself, more time to learn things I want to do. I've quit worrying about Scott's being gone. When I feel grumpy about my husband's absences, I try to remember how lucky we are he has a job he enjoys. Lots of people have situations far more difficult than ours. When the day gets hard, I give it over to the Lord. I've learned to deal with what I can and let the rest go. Scott and I have had many tough times in our marriage; it has not been easy. But we adjust. I've become more independent.

I had to find the inner strength to deal with our youngest son's Attention Deficit Disorder (ADD). Scott wasn't around to see what was going on each day. I would get calls from the school about Joshua's behavior. I knew something was wrong, but I couldn't put my finger on what it was. After two months of testing, the diagnosis was made, and I had a better idea how to work with my son. I've been the parent for the majority of our marriage.

When Scott is away, I don't sleep well because I'm responsible for everything. A woman home alone with two children hears every sound. When Scott is home he's responsible, and I sleep better. Our oldest son, Matthew, deals with his dad's absences the same way I do.

Over the years the boys and I have adjusted to Scott's being gone so much of the time. We have our routines all week, and when Scott gets home everything changes. Scott is stricter than I am, but we go by his rules when he's home.

The weeks Scott works at home, he alleviates the pressure for me by helping with the grocery shopping, laundry, and taking the boys to their activities. He'll have dinner ready for us in the evenings.

Scott goes through cycles in which he feels burned out. There are times he feels left out, too, like he's missing out on the boys growing up. Though he talks with the boys each night by phone, we all wish he were here for their special events—such as Christmas programs.

On the other hand, Scott enjoys seeing the different places on his travels. Some of his customers invite him to their homes for dinner. Scott likes to take me on trips, showing me the places he enjoys, so in the summer I go with him at least once. Scott can be very disciplined. He decided to quit drinking and smoking, and he did. He can also have high expectations of others. I came to realize I can't always live up to Scott's expectations, so I have learned to relax about it and our relationship has gotten better. I would like our son Matt to come to the same place in his relationship with his dad.

The downside of this lifestyle doesn't outweigh the positive side. I'm getting to know and like myself. And the money does make our life easier.

STRATEGY

When the travel lifestyle appears to be the best, and sometimes the only way to support the family, these strategies have helped others in the same situation.

For Husbands and Wives

- Whenever remotely possible, allow Mom to be home full-time with the children.
- Be involved in the church as a family.
- Memorize helpful Bible verses and recite them in times of stress.
- Prayerfully and responsibly invest in dependable equipment, such as vehicles and appliances. Balance time spent maintaining poorly functioning equipment against the price of replacement.
- Equip the wife with power of attorney to handle family business needs when the husband is unavailable.

For the Traveler

- Keep Christ first in your life, your family second, and your job third.

- Utilize time on the road to improve your spiritual walk through Christian teaching tapes, inspirational music, and Christian books.
- Attend church wherever you are.
- Continue to court your wife.
- Insist that the children respect their mother.
- Parent your children. Don't relegate all the parenting to your wife. When out of town, back up your wife's parenting by gently, but firmly, addressing behavior problems with your children over the phone.
- Work with your wife to solve family conflicts and challenges.
- Be sure your family has a secure place to call home.
- Develop special interests with your family, something you do together often.
- Schedule an interesting trip to coincide with holiday breaks and take the family along. Let them see what your world is like.

For the Fort Soldier

- Concentrate on the positives. Bitterness wastes your energy.
- Give your day, every day, to the Lord. Read the Psalms. Pray specifically for peace, comfort, and wisdom.
- Relax, be easier on yourself. Deal with what you can and let the rest go.
- Order pizza and don't feel guilty.
- Control the peace in the house: turn off the television, the radio, and the computer. Get to bed early.
- Read wholesome and encouraging books.
- To lower your stress level, don't overbook your time, especially when your husband is away. Allow for your husband's schedule, church, other prayerfully selected activities, and adequate rest for you and the children.
- Have a steady, trusted baby-sitter once a week so you can attend Bible study or run errands.
- Encourage your husband.

- Vent anger and frustration to your husband and a trusted friend, not to the children.
- Find support in other women who also have traveling husbands.

For the Church and Others

- The church can tape sermons and teachings for travelers to listen to on their trips.
- Get involved in truck-stop ministries.
- Listen when you need to listen. Talk when you need to talk.
- Celebrate your friend's special days.

CHAPTER TWELVE

Pain Upon Pain

"Here is my servant, whom I uphold, my chosen one in whom I delight; I will put my Spirit on him and he will bring justice to the nations. He will not shout or cry out, or raise his voice in the streets. A bruised reed he will not break, and a smoldering wick he will not snuff out."

—ISAIAH 42:1–3

W HEN I WAS NINE YEARS OLD, *my alcoholic father left home one day and never came back. In the past two years, I have also lost extended family members to death and suicide. My husband's job requires him to travel. I know intellectually that he will return from his trips. I know he is committed to me, and I trust my heavenly Father who cares for me. But emotionally, I react like that young girl who lost her daddy. When my husband walks out that door to drive to the airport, a piece of me panics. How do I really know that anyone will come back?*

—Jeri Cross

Even the healthiest marriages and families struggle with issues forced by separation. How do you survive when travel magnifies the pain of a dysfunctional past or addictive behaviors of the present? God is a gentle, loving God who calls us to cling to Him alone as we live on the edge.

TRAVEL AND ADDICTION

The following is a composite of the stories of contributors who choose to remain anonymous.

You would never guess our situation. We appear to have the perfect family life. What no one knows is that my husband is an addict—not a penniless, skid-row addict. He is a smart, successful businessman who covers his addiction well. I am equally capable of hiding the secret.

Addictions come in many forms—alcohol and drug abuse, gambling, sexual addictions (from pornography to multiple affairs to visiting prostitutes), and others. Workaholism, overeating, smoking, computer games, videos, television, and other compulsive behaviors can be equally destructive to families, but these are more "socially acceptable" addictions. We don't talk with anyone, especially anyone in the church, about the "hard-core" addictions that touch our families.

Addicts usually have more than one addictive behavior, frequently coupled with an abusive temper. Already pushed to the edge because they are living a double life, addicts readily explode. They do not enjoy their habits. They agonize over their addictions, desperately trying to stop hurting the people they love.

My husband is essentially a good man who loves his family and loves God. But he struggles with a weakness. Everyone struggles with something, but some weaknesses are more visible and destructive than others.

I discovered my husband's addiction in the first few months of our marriage. I had no idea of his struggle before we married. As a young bride, I naturally blamed myself—if I were a different person, if I were more attractive, if I could *change* something, then he wouldn't need his addiction. I believed I was inadequate and had failed him. I doubt that my esteem will ever return.

I responded as a classic codependent, and the pattern continued for almost twenty years. We discussed the problem periodically, but my husband refused to get professional help, insisting on handling his problems on his own.

I think codependency easily traps Christian women.

- We can't seem to find the balance between loving unconditionally and enabling addictive behavior. Just as Christ has forgiven us, we reach out to forgive rather than judge, knowing no sin is greater than any other. We know that pride, gossiping, and lying are just as serious in God's eyes.

- We're committed to our marriage vows. We promised to stand by our husband for life, for better or for worse.

- Our hearts are moved with compassion because we see the painful past behind the addictions and the desperate attempts to deaden that pain.

And so the cycle goes—around and around.

I worked at keeping our homelife running smoothly and not making any extra demands on my husband's life to avoid his anger. If I could "keep him happy," I could maintain a semblance of peace in our home.

I lived a nightmare. I covered the late-night hours that he was absent, never knowing when he would return. I suspected his activities but never wanted to confirm them. I pretended all was well in front of our children, family, and friends. The scary part was that I was "successful" at this masquerade. I convinced myself that as long as I could keep pretending, life would be okay.

My husband traveled as part of his business, and as time progressed the travel increased. He had absolute freedom to explore his addiction in a strange town, with no accountability to anyone. I knew it, and he knew it, but the issue had become too explosive to talk about. With that freedom, his addiction became worse.

Temptation is rampant in the travel lifestyle. Often he couldn't wait to leave town, and just as often I was relieved to see him go because the chaos in my life left with him for a few days.

Every year, with every trip, a piece of me died inside. I couldn't betray my husband by discussing our problems with our friends. My own anger turned inward, and I began drowning in depression. To keep living the lie seemed the path of least conflict. But I simply couldn't do it anymore. I decided that if my husband wouldn't get help, then I needed to. My decision threatened and angered him, but I had no choice. If I didn't get help I knew I wasn't going to survive.

During that time I clung to Jesus Christ, my only rescuer, as I always had. God had held me close through all those years, and I knew He would continue to uphold me. With the help of a compassionate counselor, I learned to let my husband's life fall apart, no longer letting myself feel responsible for his pain. In time my husband began to see the counselor and slowly discovered the past roots of his anger and addiction. He is now a recovering addict. Because of the struggles we have endured and the faithfulness of God, we now have a stronger marriage. But the road is long. It is a lifelong road. We work at our marriage and family life every day. My husband's travel schedule, mandatory in his job, brings us extra challenges, pain, and temptation.

If you are living the nightmare I lived, remember that you are not alone. Others have been there. We just don't tell each other. The pattern develops so slowly that you don't see how desperate the situation actually is. Psalm 147:3 comforts us: "He heals the brokenhearted and binds up their wounds." Get help for yourself, your husband, and your family before it is too late. Especially if your husband travels.

RECOVERING FROM ADDICTION

I had just secured my belongings on the ship when I turned to see the captain hanging a lewd pinup poster in the sleeping quarters. A familiar jolt ran through my body. Would temptation come so quickly? And from the hand of the ship's captain, my boss?

For three days I struggled with the sight of that poster. I recounted everything I had learned in a men's accountability group at church for the past six months I was home. After hiding and denying my addiction to pornography for years, I had found healing as I met with other Christian men who struggled with the same problem. In our weekly times together with our pastor, we asked each other, and God, some hard questions. We prayed together and searched the Scriptures for answers. We repented and wept together. We recommitted our bodies and thought lives to God, to our wives, and to our children. First John 1:5–9 says, "God is light; in him there is no darkness at all. If we claim to have fellowship with him yet walk in the darkness, we lie and do not live by the truth. But if we walk in the light, as he is in the light, we have fellowship with one another, and the blood of Jesus, his Son, purifies us from all sin. If we claim to be without sin, we deceive ourselves and the truth is not in us. If we confess our sins, he is faithful and just and will forgive us our sins and purify us from all unrighteousness."

For those first three days on the ship, my inner turmoil swung from victory to defeat, from hope to despair. Finally, bolstered by prayer, I approached the captain and quietly explained that the poster offended me. To my great relief, the captain said he understood and removed the poster.

While no one spoke directly to me about the incident, my shipmates made plenty of "goody-two-shoes" comments just loud enough for me to hear. How ironic. My co-workers thought I was offended because I'm a good person. If they only knew. I'm probably much worse than any of them. I thank God for one victory at a time.

THE AT-RISK WOMAN LEFT AT HOME

Addictions aren't only a "traveling man's dilemma." Women left at home can struggle with addictions too. A woman we'll call Phyllis knows the pain too well. In the early years when her husband traveled, Phyllis would drink a glass of wine in the evenings to calm her and help her sleep at night. A person who loved to be with people, she couldn't adjust to being alone.

As her husband's travel increased and her loneliness deepened, she began drinking more. She wanted to be the strong, capable wife at home, so she didn't tell her husband or anyone else about her problem. When the alcohol no longer deadened the pain, she began frequenting the local bar after work. There she met men as lonely as she was.

Phyllis never planned to have an affair. Yet one night it happened, and then it happened again. Though she played the charade of the loving, supportive wife well on the weekends, she churned in a destructive cycle of alcohol abuse and multiple affairs. Her husband suspected nothing.

Finally, no longer able to endure the 'severe depression and pain of her double life, Phyllis sought professional help. She and her husband, who no longer travels, are trying to piece their lives back together. "In repentance and rest is your salvation, in quietness and trust is your strength" (Isa. 30:15).

TRAVEL AND SURVIVAL
BY PAM HUBER

The travel lifestyle combined with raising three teens would be difficult for anyone, but for me it is a daily battle. I hide my secret well. I have agoraphobia, with a history of severe anxiety attacks and depression. Leaving my house or the area was once terrifying to me.

My husband, David, travels in blocks of two to three days; I work part-time in a local office. We have three active teenagers, and every day is hard work for me. David calls home nightly, which helps sustain our relationship. It is amazing how much the sound of his voice can calm me during those hectic days. Top priority for us is our weekly date night. Our lives start to unravel when we do not have time alone to talk.

Under a therapist's care for years, I have improved considerably. I have had to make caring for myself physically, emotionally, and spiritually a priority in my life. The healing is coming. I must be a "normal" mom for the sake of my children. David's absence pushes me to the edge of what I am capable, so I pray and call for emergency prayer from my friends. I cling to Jesus Christ. I survive the day and that is a great accomplishment.

As another friend who had agoraphobia said to me, "Our condition is a journey—not a place." There is hope. Isaiah 41:10 says, "Do not fear, for I am with you; do not be dismayed, for I am your God. I will strengthen you and help you; I will uphold you with my righteous right hand."

STRATEGY

Living on the edge is not what any of us would choose. But that is exactly where some of us find ourselves. You are not alone. There are many others on this same precipice, and most importantly Christ is there with us.

For Husbands and Wives

- Remember, your partner's addiction is not a reflection on you. You did not cause your spouse's addiction.
- If your spouse has an addiction, find a safe place and a Christian counselor whom you can talk with. Don't carry the burden alone. Get the tools you need to deal with this in a healthy manner. Prayerfully seek support. Call local pastors, Christian colleges, Christian radio stations, or Focus on the Family (Colorado Springs, CO 80995, (719) 531–5181) and request referrals for counselors or support organizations specific to your circumstances. Don't give up until you find help. Get equipped.
- Read everything you can find in the Christian realm dealing with your situation.
- If you have an addiction, get professional, godly help to overcome this problem. Don't give up if your first attempt fails. Through Christ you can live victoriously. Do it for yourself, for your spouse, and for your children.
- *Be honest.* Don't live a double life. "Secrets" lose their power when they are no longer secrets. Others struggle just like you do.
- God commands you to flee temptation. Christ is the only one who can meet all your needs.
- Arrange for an accountability relationship with someone other than your spouse.
- Stay involved in a caring church body.
- Keep your marriage your top priority. Schedule time to be together.

For the Traveler

- Stay in touch with your family.
- If you are involved in counseling, keep your appointments. Demonstrate your love for your family by diligently working to become whole again. Then help your family find wholeness as well.
- If your wife is in counseling, help her keep her appointments.
- If travel feeds an addiction, secure some form of accountability or stop traveling until you are in control.

For the Fort Soldier

- Call friends to pray with you and for you.
- Make prayer and Bible study your foundation.
- Get rest.
- Book some unwind time for you and the children.
- Keep your voice calm.
- Take each day one at a time.

For the Church And Others

- Pray diligently for the family.
- Frequently pray with your friend, either over the phone or in person.
- Ask how things are going. Be sincere.
- Offer child care while the parent goes to counseling.
- Do not cause temptation.
- As a church, face the problem honestly and straightforwardly with love.
- Compile a list of qualified counselors and support organizations. Post the list in a prominent place available to everyone in the church.
- Churches can provide serious Bible studies and host helpful seminars, workshops, and speakers dealing with tough issues such as addictions.
- Link recovered addicts with those in process.

Families Divided by Prison Walls

"When the Son of Man comes in his glory, and all the angels with him, he will sit on his throne in heavenly glory. All the nations will be gathered before him, and he will separate the people one from another as a shepherd separates the sheep from the goats. He will put the sheep on his right and the goats on his left.

"Then the King will say to those on his right, 'Come, you who are blessed by my Father; take your inheritance, the kingdom prepared for you since the creation of the world. For I was hungry and you gave me something to eat, I was thirsty and you gave me something to drink, I was a stranger and you invited me in, I needed clothes and you clothed me, I was sick and you looked after me, I was in prison and you came to visit me.'

"Then the righteous will answer him, 'Lord, when did we see you hungry and feed you, or thirsty and give you something to drink? When did we see you a stranger and invite you in, or needing clothes and clothe you? When did we see you sick or in prison and go to visit you?' The King will reply, 'I tell you the truth, whatever you did for one of the least of these brothers of mine, you did for me.' "

—MATTHEW 25:31–40

ANNE'S ALARM WOKE HER IN THE EARLY HOURS *of the morning. She slowly rolled out of bed, her body heavy in her ninth month of pregnancy. She and her young son had to drive an hour to reach San Quentin Penitentiary in time to visit her husband, who was incarcerated there.*

Dressing herself and young John, she mentally ran down the list of what the prison would not allow—no orange, blue, green, or denim clothing, nothing sheer or short, no leggings. Only her keys, identification, and money for the prison vending machines could be carried inside in a Ziplock bag.

While John slept, Anne made the long drive to the prison. She remem-

bered previous visits when armed guards escorted her handcuffed husband into a cage. After the door was locked behind him, Wayne's handcuffs were unlocked through a slot. Then Wayne would pick up the phone and talk with Anne from behind a glass barrier for thirty minutes. But today would be different. After a long fight with prison authorities, Anne had won a contact visit with Wayne.

In the predawn light, women began lining up for processing in the temporary breezeway at San Quentin. From experience, Anne was careful to avoid a fight with these women. Any offense taken out here was often carried inside, and then the men would fight. Wayne would be released soon. Involvement in a fight could increase his prison time.

At 7:30 a guard gathered IDs from the visitors and at 8:00 the women and children filed through the metal detectors.

Ushered into a cold, dirty cement corridor, Anne reminded her son not to pick at the gum on the underside of the benches while they waited another hour. After being checked again to be sure they carried only the regulated items, Anne and John were led down more halls, through electronic gates, and eventually into a large room to meet with Wayne.

Feeling tense, Anne surveyed the noisy room filled with women and children meeting prisoners: plastic chairs, vending machines, a children's video already in progress. Guards stood around the periphery. She mentally ran down the list of what the prison allowed during a contact visit with Wayne—one kiss at the beginning of the visit, one at the end; hands must be in sight at all times, arms around each other's waist only. Children under ten may sit on laps, and all children must be under control. Any violation of these rules would end their time together.

With each visit, Anne hoped things would be better between her and Wayne. Yet the emotional roller coaster that peaked at seeing him dipped low again under his relentless criticism. At the end of their time together, she drove home to face the overwhelming responsibility of providing for her family—alone.

———

Not everyone behind bars is a child molester, murderer, or bank robber. A Christian accountant, active in his church, found himself serving a one-year prison sentence for "just doing what he was told" during the savings and loan debacle a few years ago.

When a spouse goes to prison, the entire family suffers. The spouse who remains at home to hold down the fort must carry on without his or her partner's physical or financial contribution for a significant amount of time. The statistics for the survival of such a marriage are depressing.

The women who share their stories in this chapter each grew up in an abusive home. These stories leave us wishing for more positive results. They also awaken us to the struggles of a family left alone, the need for God's supernatural strength, and the importance of practical support during this time.

DRUGS, DOMESTIC VIOLENCE, AND PRISON TERMS
MORE OF ANNE'S STORY

Wayne has been in and out of prison since he was fifteen years old. Incarcerated five times in the five years of our marriage, he has been gone more than he's been home, a round robin of drugs, domestic violence, and prison terms. When he was incarcerated, Wayne would tell me, "Baby, baby, I love you. I'll never leave you." But then he would be released and run off and do it all again.

I quit asking why, but I really have a hard time trusting God. Wayne and I both have emotional scars from our past and need healing. Because I was abused as a child, I desperately want to stop the generational pattern with my sons.

When Wayne went to prison, I found myself spending too much time dwelling on our situation, so I went to work to provide for my sons. Men behind bars are very insecure. Wayne accused me of flirting with men at work. Anytime he called home collect and I didn't answer, he accused me of being unfaithful.

As the wife of an inmate, I wonder where I fit socially. I'm a married woman, yet in some ways it seems like I'm not. I can't attend the church singles group, and yet I feel awkward with the married couples. Fellowship with other church families is vital, but couples with a less-than-secure marriage perceive me as a threat. Wayne is jealous of the men in the church who try to provide a healthy male role model for my boys while their dad is locked up.

Society rejects my children and me, so we need Christ's unconditional love and the acceptance and nurturing of other Christians and the church. They have fixed my car and my broken windows, given us groceries, shared garden vegetables, handed down clothes for my children, and helped with finances. The best help a church can give to families of inmates is to minister to them, not just hand them everything. Don't let them "play the system." Invite them to be a regular part of the church.

The area where I need the most help is with my children. It was traumatic for my youngest son to see his father arrested, handcuffed, and taken away. Danny needs lots of prayer. I must continually tell him that I will never leave him or stop loving him.

Behind bars Wayne has no responsibility. All his decisions are made for him. He gets so dependent on that lifestyle, he can't choose a soda on his own.

Prison life also breeds self-centeredness. When he's home, Wayne expects me to make all the meals, do all the cleaning, keep the kids out of his way, and be available to him at all times. He's looking for a savior, a woman to love him enough to make everything okay. Instead of lifting my burden, he's like having another child in the home. Wayne has unreal expectations that I can't meet. He gets pushed around in prison, so he vents his anger and frustrations at home by pushing us around.

The very strength that holds our home together while Wayne is in prison is exactly what he criticizes me for when he's home. I make all the day-to-day decisions when he's gone, but this is not a natural role for me. I want Wayne to be the head of the household. If he would show me I can trust him, I would gladly hand it all over to him.

One verse that holds me together is "Be still, and know that I am God" (Ps. 46:10). I also cling to 2 Corinthians 1:3–5, 10–11, which says, "Praise be to the God and Father of our Lord Jesus Christ, the Father of compassion and the God of all comfort, who comforts us in all our troubles, so that we can comfort those in any trouble with the comfort we ourselves have received from God. For just as the sufferings of Christ flow over into our lives, so also through Christ our comfort overflows. On him we have set our hope that he will continue to deliver us, as you help us by your prayers. Then many will give thanks on our behalf for the gracious favor granted us in answer to the prayers of many."

Someday I'll be able to help someone else. Sin increases. Prison numbers go up. More women are battered and bruised. They will need someone who has been through it to help them. In the meantime, my children and I must put on the full armor of God.

DEPENDING ON THE LORD
KAREN'S STORY

I wish I could go out to dinner and have my husband escort me, but he's not here. He's in prison.

I was waitressing at a truck stop when I met and married Franklin. He had a seven-year-old son, Frankie. After our son, Charles, was born, I left Franklin because of his drugs. One weekend I took Charles to visit his dad and Franklin talked me into staying. We had another child, Jami Elaine.

I've always felt left out of Franklin's life because I didn't do the things he did. He'd be out until 4:00 A.M., or would be gone for three or four days. We moved often because we couldn't pay the rent. We lived in a motel for six months, and a couple of raunchy apartments. They were all shacks.

At the time of Franklin's first criminal charges, we were homeless. He totaled the car, severely damaged his back, and went to prison. It all happened at the same time. I nursed him after his back surgery—giving him his bath, helping him up to walk to the bathroom. I've always been there for him, but he's never been there for me.

The second charges against Franklin were felony charges, and Charles (then eight) and Jami (age six) were dragged out of our home by authorities. The children were so traumatized when they were returned six days later that they just clung to me. They didn't even want to go to school.

With Franklin in prison, I applied for welfare. Out of the $694 I received each month, $575 went for rent. I still needed to pay for electricity, food, clothes for the children, and other living expenses. Collect calls from Franklin amounted to $100 every month. Each time I visited him, it cost another $40 for gas, the required packaged food, or expensive food from the prison vending machines.

Additionally, wives were advised to support their husbands by sending a package every three months. The packages contained new jeans, underclothes, personal items, and treats. I let bills go and fell behind financially in order to provide these extras for Frank. He had a roof over his head, utilities, clothes, and food, while I was giving up necessities for myself and the children. Finally I realized I had to quit sending these "extras" for Franklin so I could give the children what they needed.

My first visit to San Quentin scared me to death. Guards were blowing whistles and firing guns to control unruly inmates. Another prisoner's wife threatened me with a gun, and I was afraid my children would have to grow up without a father *or* a mother.

Family visits lasted three nights and four days. I was allowed to take three sets of clothes and packaged food. Guards searched everything. The trailers where we stayed had one butcher knife chained to the counter, plates, forks, pots and pans, and see-through curtains. There was a play area for the children. Armed guards stood at each corner of the compound, checking periodically to see that the prisoners didn't escape.

At every visit I cried. I always had to reassure Franklin of my faithfulness, though he was the one who was guilty. It was always "pity me because I'm in prison," but I couldn't do anything right. His accusations made the children suspicious of me.

Franklin's imprisonment has deeply affected the children. Charles' grades dropped to Fs—though he is doing better now. My daughter's anger comes out in fighting at school. The children need constant prayer. It's hard doing the parenting by myself, keeping a roof over our heads, and providing for the children.

Though I had been a Christian from childhood, I rededicated my life to the Lord when Frank went to prison. Charles and Jami had already been going to Bible study through a local church that sent a van around to pick them up. I found help from some support groups. For the three middle years of Franklin's prison term, I attended a group for husbands and wives at San Quentin. I also got involved with Kairos Outside, a support group for wives and mothers of inmates. I felt so abandoned. I needed someone to hug me and tell me they loved me and couldn't make it without me. Kairos made me feel I was somebody.

At the Kairos retreat I learned to exercise spiritual warfare over the things in my home. Jeremiah 29:11 tells me I have a future, " 'For I know the plans I have for you,' declares the Lord, 'plans to prosper you and not to harm you, plans to give you hope and a future.' " God opened my eyes. I wouldn't be as close to Him if I hadn't gone through all this.

I depend on Christ for my strength. Isaiah 40:31 says, "But those who hope in the Lord will renew their strength. They will soar on wings like eagles; they will run and not grow weary, they will walk and not be faint."

After five years in prison, Franklin was released. It would have been better for him to have gone first to a halfway house to transition back into society before he came home. He was extremely critical of me and the children, and he had a temper. I couldn't stand to let him discipline the children. Frank stayed in the house, afraid of getting into trouble and winding up back in jail. He wouldn't even go to get his driver's license. He ran up all kinds of bills, dirtied up the house, and never did anything to help. Frank felt God had let him down, and he gave up on the Lord.

He would watch television or play Nintendo until four in the morning, then sleep until 11:00 A.M. The children and I had to tiptoe around the house so we wouldn't get hollered at. After six months with Frank home, I couldn't take it anymore. I felt so betrayed and hurt I couldn't sleep in the same bed with him. I was dying inside. The social worker ordered Frank out of the house, and he went to a homeless shelter for three weeks until he moved in with a man who ministers in the prisons.

I filed for divorce the next month, but every radio and television show and every Sunday sermon I heard said God hated divorce and He could work out anything. My Christian aunt and uncle and others in the church suggested a legal separation. I wanted to be married. I wanted my children to have both their parents because I don't have mine. I tell my kids I only want the best for them and I know they can make it.

Frank began counseling, and we've been working on our relationship. But I keep seeing the old patterns return. I keep hearing the same excuses.

Over the years the church has provided financial help, car maintenance, friendship, and "family" for me and my children. Sometimes a family in the church will take Charles to a ball game or buy him a new outfit or shoes. Though Frank never wanted to go to church with the children and me, my pastor paid weekly visits to Frank in the county jail and wrote to him. One thing I am truly grateful for is that the Lord has provided a house for the children and me through government-subsidized housing. The house is very nice; it is the first place I've lived that had a yard with grass.

Through it all, God gives me Scriptures at different times. Psalm 3:5–6 says, "I lie down and sleep; I wake again, because the Lord sustains me. I will not fear the tens of thousands drawn up against me on every side."

Right now, I'm living day to day. I don't like myself; I'm lonely and hurting inside. I was never able to do the things I wanted to do—to be a deputy sheriff, a highway patrolperson, or a postal worker. I hope to be able to look ahead to the future. God keeps telling me I only need to please Him. Lately others have commented that they hear me whistling and see me smiling more. They say they see growth in my life and admire all I've gone through. The only thing that's helped me through it all is the Lord.

For me, this marriage has been nothing but sixteen years of heartache. I know God will allow no more than I can handle, but I often ask, "Isn't this enough?"

FROM PRISON TO PULPIT
BY SAM HUDDLESTON

Pastor of Lighthouse Covenant Church in Benicia, California, and former president of Match–2 Prison Ministries, Sam Huddleston and his wife, Linda, have three grown children. As an ex-felon, Sam has experienced the prison issue from both sides. Here are his observations:

Maintaining strong family ties and contact with the community is the best insurance that a prisoner will not be a repeat offender. Yet we still build prisons in the woods, making it nearly impossible for families to visit. That's buying into Hitler's principle of getting rid of the undesirables. It's a travesty for politicians to prey on people's fears.

I'm not soft on crime. People can get angry and bitter, but life is too short and precious for that. I only have so much energy; I have to focus it on the positive. Prisoners entering the prison need to hear, "I believe you can change. You committed a horrible crime and you're going to serve your time, but I believe you can change." My dad kept telling me I was going to be a great man. We all have value. Nothing is more powerful than words. Bullets kill. Words make killers.

When a husband is sentenced to prison, his wife feels betrayed. She goes through all the stages that a person experiences when there is a death, except it doesn't end. She feels denial, anger, and then acceptance. He's embarrassed and sometimes doesn't want his family to see him in prison. It's difficult to have a stable home when the man is in the house, but when one of the partners is taken out of the house, it's major miracle time. Some marriages make it, but not many do.

Prison represents broken dreams and the dreams of the people who were broken to get there. Negative situations pull out what's in you, but jail has nothing to do with that. You learn to adjust. Time does not heal all wounds; you merely learn to live with that gaping hole.

For the spouse in jail, get into the Word. And get into prison Bible study. You must want Jesus more than your freedom. Jesus is the only one who is there with you. There is no one else in the world who can meet your needs.

Loneliness is the biggest factor for prisoners and their families. They want someone to fill that void. Reaching out to prisoners and their families is an ongoing ministry. Prison chaplains offer Bibles, Bible studies, Christian reading material, and someone to talk to. Counseling is available for inmates and their spouses to help the marriage and to assist in the prisoner's transition back into the home upon release.

The children need your presence—to hold their hand and to fill the void. It's good for men to pal up with their children. It costs $80 million to operate San Quentin Penitentiary for one year. It costs $20 thousand per man for one year, $25 thousand per woman, and $31 thousand for a youth. The age rate of prisoners has dropped in recent years. We can either pay now or pay later.

Strategy

Families divided by prison walls have unique needs. Here are practical helps for those in this situation, and those seeking to help.

For Husbands and Wives

- Be aware that the prison experience can push your already strained marriage relationship to the breaking point. Trust God to be your source, security, a very present help in time of trouble. Go to the Lord daily, continually, in prayer. Seek your strength in His Word.
- Face the reality of your present situation and make plans to fix what you can.
- Communicate as often as possible, but be careful not to wound each other with criticism or blame.
- Plug into a ministering church and parachurch organizations such

as Prison Fellowship, PO Box 17500, Washington, DC 20041-0500, (703) 478–0100.

- Provide your children with as much security as possible.
- Teach your children to have faith in God. Help them understand that the Lord always offers forgiveness and hope.

For the Spouse in Prison

- Use the time you are incarcerated wisely. Focus on God. Desire Him more than freedom.
- Ask God to help you in your loneliness. He is right there with you. There is no one else in the world who can meet your needs.
- Admit your shortcomings and seek forgiveness and healing from the Lord.
- Take honest stock of your situation and make the necessary improvements in your spiritual walk and your relationship with your wife and children.
- Set healthy goals for the future and pursue them.
- Attend prison chapel services regularly. Take advantage of Bible studies, counseling, parenting classes, and other enriching programs provided through the prison or by correspondence.
- Daily spend time in Bible reading and prayer, especially praying for your family.
- Keep in touch with your wife, children, family, church, friends, and community.
- Encourage your wife and children through your words and example.
- Find positive and creative ways to care for your wife and children even from prison.
- Express sincere appreciation when your wife and children make the effort to visit you.

For the Fort Soldier

- Immerse yourself in the Word of God. Spend daily time in prayer and Bible study.
- Be active in a local Bible-believing church. The Lord will be your

strength and wisdom through this.

- In addition to church fellowship, take advantage of Christian marriage and parenting support groups. Look to God to heal your marriage and family.
- Surround yourself with caring and supportive friends.
- Be honest about your situation with yourself, your spouse, your children, and others.
- Focus on the positive; things *will* change.
- Watch for signs of God at work in your life; watch for the miracles and great plans He has in store for you.

For the Church and Others

- Pray for the family regularly. Be an encourager.
- Allow the spouse at home to minister as a functioning part of the church body. Be sensitive to the family's need "to fit" socially.
- Do not expect people's circumstances to stay the same. People and circumstances change.
- Do not tempt someone to stumble.
- Help where you can in terms of household maintenance, car repairs, baby-sitting, providing groceries, putting gas in the car, paying a utility bill. Share gently used clothing, garden vegetables, and favorite books.
- Invite the family over for holidays, dinner, a picnic, or a video and popcorn.
- Sponsor a child in Little League, music lessons, summer camp, college courses, or other enriching activities. Send the children a subscription to a Christian magazine. Schedule time to play baseball, teach sewing, or visit the library together.
- Disciple the youngsters in their Christian walk.
- Take the children to church when the parent cannot.
- As a church, help the family financially and, if applicable, help them find employment.
- Gather laypeople to provide counseling and classes on spiritual growth, parenting, marriage, and finances at the church facility and in the prisons.

- The church can provide space for prison ministries and organize visitation to the prison. Keep in touch with the prisoner by phone and letters. Aid the inmate in his spiritual walk through Bibles and Christian resources. Encourage the inmate to find ways to maintain his responsibilities as head of his household and to serve as a missionary within the prison walls.
- Welcome former prisoners into church fellowship.
- Help the former inmate find employment upon his release.
- Realize helping families whose lives are affected by prison terms is an ongoing ministry.

Is Travel Right for You?

As iron sharpens iron, so one man sharpens another.

For lack of guidance a nation falls, but many
advisers make victory sure.

"Suppose one of you wants to build a tower. Will he not first sit down
and estimate the cost to see if he has enough money to complete it? For
if he lays the foundation and is not able to finish it, everyone who sees
it will ridicule him, saying, 'This fellow began to build and was not able
to finish.'

"Or suppose a king is about to go to war against another king. Will
he not first sit down and consider whether he is able with ten thousand
men to oppose the one coming against him with twenty thousand? If he
is not able, he will send a delegation while the other is still a long way
off and will ask for terms of peace."

—*PROVERBS 27:17; 11:14; LUKE 14:28–32*

D R. *JAMES DOBSON WROTE IN HIS BOOK,* Dr. Dobson Answers Your
Questions, *"For the husband who appreciates the willingness of
his wife to stand against the tide of public opinion—staying home in her
empty neighborhood in the exclusive company of jelly-faced toddlers and
strong-willed adolescents—it is about time he gave her some help.*

*"I'm not merely suggesting that he wash the dishes or sweep the floor.
I'm referring to the provision of emotional support . . . of conversation . . .
of making her feel like a lady . . . of building her ego . . . of giving her one
day of recreation each week . . . of taking her out to dinner . . . of telling*

her that he loves her. Without these armaments, she is left defenseless against the foes of the family—the foes of his family!"[1]

MAKING THE BIG DECISION

Late Wednesday evening the phone rang.

"Hello."

"PeggySue, this is Bob Quinn. I've been offered a job with some travel involved. I called to ask you and Keith some questions before Kathleen and I make our decision."

More and more people are facing similar decisions. It's a job offer—a promotion, actually. The position is lucrative. The travel sounds exciting and glamorous. Do you take the job?

In terms of responsibility and compensation, Bob Quinn has already hit the ceiling in his present position. He is "topped out," or unpromotable. The new job would offer new challenges, new learning experiences, as well as opportunities for career and monetary growth. The new position also requires a commute and travel, reducing the time Bob has with his family. Bob and Kathleen have seven children, including four under the age of four and one special-needs child.

Another couple, Dale and Lynne, pondered a similar job offer requiring extended travel. Their children were grown and independent, and Lynne could accompany Dale on trips if she wanted to come along. Together they would see new parts of the country.

Before accepting a job that requires travel, many factors should be considered.

- Travel usually comes into play in the middle-management level of the corporate environment. This is also the level at which employees are most easily expendable. Companies frequently cut back at this level because they have to or want to. Middle-management workers often feel a need to be constantly on guard,

[1] *Dr. James Dobson's Focus on the Family Bulletin*, vol. 6, no. 5, June 1993 (published by Tyndale House Publishers, Carol Stream, IL, in cooperation with Focus on the Family, Colorado Springs, CO.) All rights reserved.

expending maximum effort to get the notice of management.

- When climbing the corporate ladder, your time is not your own. With the title of manager comes the responsibility to do whatever it takes to get the job done, and the job is never done. The pressure comes home with you. Weigh what you will have to give up to accommodate the extra hours on the job.

- Corporate America is not particularly family-oriented. Accepting a middle- or upper-management position, or any position with a heavy travel schedule, should be a mutual decision between husband and wife. Balance the costs both in time and effort with the needs of your family. It takes determination to work smart within the designated workday in order to reserve time and energy for family. It requires commitment to stand against pressure that equates overtime with loyalty to the job, and after hours at the desk with setting a good example for fellow workers.

- Understand your responsibilities and authority before accepting the job. Get vacation time, compensation for travel time, and bonus schedules in writing.

- To be sure the company is financially stable, ask to review their financial report. It's your responsibility to know as much about the company as possible, not only financially, but market share, future potential, growth potential, and competition.

- Does management recognize that employees have a family life that must be maintained during off-hours? During the interview process, be up front about your family situation. For one dad that meant letting his company know he had a commitment to coach his sons' ice hockey team, which made him unavailable for after-hour meetings on Mondays.

- Consider the location of the new job. Commuting steals time from your homelife. If the upcoming travel will be by airplane, how far away is the airport?

- Decide what you and your family need and want in a job. Look beyond your monetary needs. Consider taking a leave of absence from your present job to try the second one on for size. It's okay to take a chance and try something new, but know what your reasons are. Often, once you start down the road of a travel-oriented job, the only speed is acceleration.

- Husbands, listen to your wife's concerns, fears, and counsel. God can speak to you through your spouse. Keep in mind that your wife's security is found primarily in a loving relationship with you, not in your career or your paycheck.

- Consider your importance in the home. Consistency in your work schedule may be important to your wife and your children. Your help and strength is needed to nurture the children, run the home, and provide spiritual leadership through regular family devotions. That's how it was for a woman named Debbie. For years her husband, Russ, worked on call as a tugboat operator. "We can never plan anything," she said. "We never know when his beeper will call him to the boat. The children are always looking over their shoulder to see if their dad is still here."

For the wife, we cannot think of one benefit from her husband's traveling. Monetary rewards rarely compensate for the load placed on her shoulders. She is responsible for it all—the children, the wakeful nights, the fevers, the homework, the housework, the yard work, the meals, the phone calls, the shopping, and the errands; killing the spiders, taking out the trash, paying the bills, locking the doors, conducting family devotions, and tucking everyone into bed at night. Most wives prefer their husband's involvement with the family over the slightly higher paycheck that may (or may not) come with the travel lifestyle.

It is flattering to be wooed by a company, to have a prospective employer offer you the moon. Think through your decision with a clear head. List the pros and cons of your present job and the prospective job. Carefully weigh each aspect against your family's needs and temperaments. The job, after all, is a tool you use to care for your family. Your job and the work done there will all burn up one day, amounting to only meaningless vanity and a striving after the wind. Your family is eternal. Keep your perspective.

In Dale and Lynne's case, they weighed the ramifications of a job requiring extended travel and decided it was a great opportunity. There were no pressing responsibilities to hold Dale close to home.

On the other hand, at his current job Bob has a collection of sick leave and has earned maximum vacation time. He works close enough to home to stop in at lunchtime or run home if a crisis arises. When their baby, Michael, became seriously ill at a few weeks of age, Bob was able to take time off from work to care for the children at home while Kathleen stayed in the hospital with their infant.

Ecclesiastes 3:1 reminds us, "There is a time for everything, and a season for every activity under heaven." After much prayer and discussion, Bob and Kathleen decided Bob's current position was best for their present situation. "Right now Kathleen and the children need me as close as I can be and at home as often as possible," Bob stated.

COMING HOME
ONE SOLUTION TO THE TRAVEL CHALLENGE

Weighing the pros and cons of your current travel lifestyle and its effects on your family may suggest a change. One obvious solution to the travel challenge is to stop. Come home. Make adjustments in the job or change jobs. And certainly this book would not be complete without offering examples of families who have done just that.

MAJOR LEAGUE HUSBAND AND FATHER
TIM AND CHRISTINE BURKE'S STORY

Tim Burke made the headlines on February 27, 1993, when he opted to trade his six-figure contract with the Cincinnati Reds in favor of being a major league husband and father.

At thirty-four years old, Burke was in the prime of his career and fulfilling his lifetime dream—pitching in the major leagues.

"What I was thinking about was blowing me away," Tim described. "I was surprised by the fact that I was seriously thinking about retiring from baseball. Christine and I had talked about it, and we decided that I wanted to play another year for sure. I worked out and worked out and I was in the greatest shape ever. Got down to spring training and went to the first day of practice and from the minute I got my uniform on I was just thinking the whole time, *What am I doing here?* My heart and my passion was with my family. They'd always been a high priority, but I still had that passion for baseball. But now the heart and the passion was with Christine and the kids. I struggled with that for a few days, and I just knew I was not peaceful on the ball field."

Tim said, "I can change my mind, but only God can change my heart and that's what happened. My heart was with my family, and I did not want to put Christine through another year of being mom and dad and mover and everything else. It was all on her shoulders because I was gone so much."

Christine's heart had been moving in that direction for two years. "After we adopted our third child, Nicole, and all the things we went through with her open-heart surgery, it started to put such a strain on the family that I felt we needed to just be home and be together. But I could see that Tim still wanted to play, and it would have been premature if he were to retire. I think this timing was absolutely perfect."

She continued, "I could accept the fact that Tim had retired for the children, and I had freely expressed my gratitude to God as well as to Tim for his love and commitment as a father. But what struck me full force was that he had done it for me, Christine. Not just for the children. For me."

Tim related, "I retired to invest my time into my family, which I wasn't going to be able to do if I played baseball another year. It was the perfect way I could tell and show Christine how much I loved her. I'm the only father these children have, and I'm the only husband my wife has. They need me an awful lot more than baseball does. Baseball has kept rolling just fine without me. But without me these children are going to be damaged because children need their parents. I want to be that role model for my little boys to learn from to grow up to be men of God. And I want to be there to be the loving father for my daughters. You can't even compare that investment to the money I would have made in baseball."

Christine observed, "We forget how important the father is. I am a lot to the children: I'm their mommy, I'm stability, I can see the importance I have in their lives. But then I can see the importance that Tim has on them. The day before he retired, he told the children that night, and I will never forget Stephanie. She's only five and a half years old, but she looked up at Tim and she just said, 'Daddy, thank you for loving me so much.' Little Ryan jumped up and down and said, 'This is great news, Daddy!' Sometime later, a lady asked Ryan what his daddy did for a living and Ryan said, 'Well, he used to play baseball, but he quit because he loves me so much.' Already, what an impression it has made."

"We can say how much our family means to us all we want, but the only thing that's going to stick, and the only thing that's going to be remembered is what we do," Tim emphasized. "Hopefully I'm going to be able, with Christine, to raise our children the way God wants them to be raised. And then they're going to think back and know that we just didn't talk about it, we did it. I pray that my children will know the commitment that we've put into them, and then that's going to carry on to their children, and their children, and that's how things are going to change."

The Burkes have avoided extravagant living and invested prudently. As their family grows, Tim and Christine have learned, "If all you want is what the Lord wants, then what you want is usually what the Lord wants. We can trust God if we let Him have control. That brings to light Psalm 37:4, "Delight yourself in the Lord and he will give you the desires of your heart."

Christine said, "We realized that what we had been doing was surviving instead of thriving. If we want the kind of family we desire in our hearts, it's going to mean sacrifice, and it meant walking away from something Tim loved. Like Tim has said, all we ever ate was bread, that's all we ever tasted, and that's fine. But suddenly we tasted cake, and we desired that because in our relationship we started to become much more intimate. Once baseball started again with spring training, that intimacy was put on hold again because of all the travel. We want to help other couples do the best job they can so they don't have to prematurely retire."[2]

FOLLOWING IN DAD'S FOOTSTEPS
DR. JAMES DOBSON'S STORY

When Dr. James Dobson, author and president of Focus on the Family, decided the nationwide traveling required to present seminars was not worth the cost to his family, he was actually following in the footsteps of his own father. Here are his recollections:

There are so many people out there who are just existing. Some people don't have the ability to change that, but others do. I want to address those people who have been thinking about the concerns they have in their own families and ask, when are you going to deal with it? Are you going to wait until your kids are grown? Is there some station down there someplace that your train is moving toward and then you'll get it together? Wouldn't it be better to address it now if it's possible to do so, and put your family at a higher level of priority?

When I was a junior in high school, I was sixteen years old and I'd been a good kid. I hadn't gotten into what used to be called "out broken sin." I never did terrible things. But I was beginning to get a little rebellious and beginning to kinda push the limits.

My father was gone a lot. He was a prominent evangelist in our denomination and was booked four years in advance. And when he saw this, I mean, in one day, he canceled that whole slate—four years—sold our house, moved the family 700 miles away, and took a church, a pastorate, so that he could be at home with me my last two years of high school.

We fished together, we hunted together. He made an incredible professional sacrifice, even affecting his ministry, in order to put his family at the highest level of priorities. When people hear me talk about him today, it sounds like I make a saint out of him—he wasn't. He was a very ordinary man who loved his family and loved his God.

---

[2]Tim and Christine Burke, *Major League Dad* (Colorado Springs, Colo.: Focus on the Family).

It's because of those key decisions he made in my childhood to put his family at a high level of priorities, and my love for the Lord, that my desire to emulate him and to carry on his work and to propagate his values can be traced to those things.

Engraved on the footstone of James Dobson Sr. are two words: 'He prayed.' When I reach the end of my days, just a moment or two from now, I must look back on something more meaningful than the pursuit of houses and land and machines and stocks and bonds. Nor is fame of any lasting benefit. I will consider my earthly existence to have been wasted unless I can recall a loving family, a consistent investment in the lives of people, and an earnest attempt to serve God, who made me. Nothing else makes sense.

Years ago we were engaged in a film series called *Focus on the Family*. At that time I was trying to make a decision about the conflict between the ministry and the message that I wanted to get out and the need to stay home with my own children. I've done a lot of dumb things in my life, but I think the smartest thing I ever did was to stay home and watch my kids grow up.

The conclusion I've drawn that outranks all others is that nothing in life matters except love for God and His son, Jesus Christ, and love for mankind beginning with my own family. This is why I've been home these years, because these years are passing so fast and I wanted to be there to have that influence on my kids, see them grow up, and to instill these values that I care about.

The years have passed so rapidly. I have valued those years with my kids so much and by being home these past years I have their childhood videotaped in my mind. I've got it here in my mind because I was home to see it, and I'm thankful for that.[3]

THE REST OF THE STORY
AN INTERVIEW WITH BILL KARLIK

Though Debbie and Bill Karlik's story began in chapter four, it continues here. Employed with a major oil company for fourteen years,

---

[3]Dr. James Dobson, *A Father Looks Back* (Dallas, Tex.: Word, Inc., 1986). All rights reserved.

Bill began a process of career changes to bring him home more. Here's what happened:

I spent two and a half years in field training where I was gone 75 percent of the time. I liked what I did but I hated being away from home. So I took a job in San Francisco at corporate headquarters. I didn't like the corporate world, but I was off the road. I decided to try to handle it, but it just didn't work well. I sold my soul to the corporate world. I wondered if my family was getting the best part of me, or only the leftovers.

In addition to the demands of the corporate realm, my commute stole an additional three hours each day from my family. I didn't care about a career, I wanted to be an active parent, but you have to be around to do that. I sensed from Debbie that the situation was not good for her. I could have survived it, but being apart left most of the burden on her. We discussed it some, but not much.

I knew my current circumstances kept me from being an effective husband and father. I needed to do whatever I could to have time with my family. I'm an intricate part of my family, and I have to be there. One thing that stuck in my mind was a quote from Tim Hansel's book *What Kids Need Most in a Dad*: "Kids don't understand quality time, only quantity time."

In November of 1993, I caught my boss in the hall and asked to speak with him. We talked in his office for about twenty minutes. My speech was not planned; I let the Lord tell me what to say when I was spilling my guts. I told my boss my family is important to me and I needed to be home more. I said I was open to relocating out of state.

From a corporate standpoint my boss was not pleased, but from a personal standpoint he understood. He explained the company was in the midst of redeployment, so it was not a favorable time for a change. I knew I had done what I needed to do. The rest was up to the Lord. Debbie was pleasantly surprised that evening when I told her what had transpired.

Two months later, I was given a new position as Operations Supervisor in Louisville, Kentucky. A lateral career move, the new job required minimal travel averaging two days per month. The move allowed us to purchase land a mere fifteen-minute drive from my office and build a home near extended family.

We experienced joy and sorrow together. We would be moving closer to extended family, but it was hard to think of leaving friends in California.

Our house sold in March, and two weeks later I flew to Kentucky to begin my new position. Debbie remained behind so our children could finish the school year. She and the two older children, ages eleven and nine, moved in with friends from church. The two younger children, ages five and three, went to stay with Debbie's parents in Ohio, where I joined them each weekend.

It was not ideal, it was not even a good situation. But it was temporary. On July 4 the family reunited in Kentucky, where we stayed with relatives until our home was completed in the fall.

In a marriage there are going to be rough times, but they aren't as rough when you work through them together. Because I've seen the importance of a good marriage, I want to stress to my children the importance of finding the mate God has for each of them should He call them to be married. Being home allows me to be involved with my children's spiritual development. I talk about the Lord with my children. I ask how they're doing with the Lord—did they remember to pray that day? Sometimes the answer is no, and I appreciate that honesty. In the ease of conversation, I let them know the Lord is important. Once the children have accepted Christ as their Lord, it's a privilege to nurture that flame. I use Bible memory and quiet time to build my spiritual armor. I'm not as consistent as I should be, but I keep working at it and God is gracious to keep me on track.

We need to fight the thought that we're only successful if we're doing something great in the corporate world. If you feel you don't have enough time with your family, you probably don't. Look at what you can do to invest more in your family. Then trust God's promises to take care of you and them.

EPILOGUE

Actually, our epilogue should be quite simple: Bill, Debbie, and their four wonderful, marvelous, and talented children (who love the Lord and have all given their life to Jesus) moved to Louisville, Kentucky, and lived happily ever after.

However, since I am writing this from Angarsk, Russia (East Siberia), that's not quite how the story goes.

Our family enjoyed ten good months together in our new home. I got home from work about 3:30 P.M. each day, attended my children's sporting activities, and had lots of time with Debbie, my best friend.

We lived close to my mom, sister, brother, and Debbie's parents, but I soon realized that my family's hearts were back in California with our closest friends. I felt that through time and prayer, we would adjust.

One day my boss asked if I would be interested in a short-term assignment to Russia.

My initial response was, "No, but tell me about it anyhow." The assignment fit with my work background, and after much prayer, Debbie and I decided to accept the position for three reasons. First, at the end of this assignment I have a good chance of being relocated back to San Francisco. Second, for every nine weeks spent in Angarsk, I spend four weeks of uninterrupted time at home with my family. Third, the salary differential allows us to pay off some bills while Debbie stays home full-time with the children.

Even as I sit here, fifty miles from the middle of nowhere, I sense that God has yet another epilogue on our horizon. I have been experiencing a growing desire to go into the ministry full-time. I pray that if God does call me into full-time ministry I will be smart enough, faithful enough, and submissive enough to answer on the first ring.

STRATEGY

If coming home—spending less time on the road for business travel—is your goal, here are some suggestions that helped these families make their lifestyle changes.

For Husbands and Wives

- Pray about your decision.
- Place your family at a high level of priority.
- If you feel the Lord prompting you to make a change, explore your options. If you can make the change, do it. Don't wait until the children are grown.
- Discuss the option of doing with less in exchange for having Dad be a larger part of the family.
- To reduce the financial pressure, avoid extravagant living and invest prudently.

For the Traveler

- If you feel like you don't have enough time with your family, consider what changes you *can* make.
- Tell your boss about your goal to be away from the family less often. Ask if adjustments can be made in the job or if there is another suitable position within the company.
- Consider early retirement as an option.
- Don't trade travel for other activities that take you from your family. Spend lots of time with your wife and children. Build a strong relationship with those most precious to you. Be a dynamic influence in the lives of your children.
- Consider juggling your work schedule to allow more time at home. For example, work earlier in the day to keep your family evenings intact. Locating closer to the job will save commute time.
- Be aware of the effect your absence has on your home.
- Talk casually and often to your children about their spiritual walk.

For the Fort Soldier

- Gently express your desires for your spouse to be home. Prayerfully wait on the Lord to work a change in your husband's heart and your family's lifestyle.
- Realize that leaving the travel lifestyle is a gift to you from your spouse.

- Be prepared for some inconvenience during the adjustment period that may accompany your husband's job change.
- Exercise your sense of humor.

For the Church and Others

- If you know of a suitable position that may suit a traveler's goal to be home more frequently, pass on that information.
- Encourage the family as they make adjustments.
- Open your home to host the family if they need temporary living accommodations during relocation.

CHAPTER FIFTEEN

Advice From the Veterans

> Then I realized that it is good and proper for a man to eat and drink, and to find satisfaction in his toilsome labor under the sun during the few days of life God has given him—for this is his lot. Moreover, when God gives any man wealth and possessions, and enables him to enjoy them, to accept his lot and be happy in his work—this is a gift from God. He seldom reflects on the days of his life, because God keeps him occupied with gladness of heart.
>
> —*ECCLESIASTES 5:18–20*

T WENTY YEARS AGO, AS I WAS FLYING HOME *from a grueling business trip, an older man seated next to me asked me about my family. I explained that I had a wife and two young children waiting for me at home. We discussed our common sales profession. Then he asked, "What will you do when you get home?"*

I replied, "I am exhausted. . . . I will crash."

"Son," he advised, "if you want your marriage to work, you can't do that. Your wife is your best customer. She is as exhausted as you are from the long week alone with the children. Take your wife out. Wine and dine her. Bring her flowers. Make her feel special. She is your last and most important customer of the week."

I have no idea if the man spoke from experience, if he had a successful marriage, or had paid the price of a divorce. But I took his advice to heart.

—Ed Kientz

The following stories come from women whose husbands traveled their entire married lives. They raised children. Their marriages survived. What did they do right? What do they wish they had done differently?

ED'S BEST CUSTOMER
CHARILYN KIENTZ'S STORY

Ed and I married early in life. We were, and still are, very much in love. Ed's sales position required him to travel throughout our entire marriage, often for two to three weeks at a stretch. I have never known any other life. The early years were wonderful and romantic. As a young bride, I enjoyed traveling with Ed to exciting places.

But then life changed. We had two young children, and I needed to be home with them. I felt very much alone. In those days, I did not know even one other woman who had a traveling spouse.

I desperately missed my husband but tried to focus on parenting our children. We decided to celebrate and include the children in Ed's travel; there was no point in pretending that it wasn't a major part of our lives. We took him to the airport so our children would understand where he was going. We greeted Ed at the airport when he returned with "welcome home" signs and surprised him with homecoming parties. Ed brought the children presents and had funny stories to share about his travels in unique places.

THE NEGATIVE SIDE

- Our airport trips became less frequent as our children became older and had homework commitments. When Ed began traveling internationally, his flight schedules were unpredictable. No longer able to meet him at the airport, we would leave a candle burning in the window for his late-night arrivals home. It was our symbol that we were waiting for him.
- Our children handled Ed's travel better than I did. I am not someone who likes to be alone. I was *so lonely*. It was especially difficult when he was absent on my birthday or our anniversary or special

school events for the children. I would often just show up with my children on friends' doorsteps, hoping they would invite us in. I dreaded going home to that empty house. I prayed that someone would invite us over for dinner.

- Church functions were rarely comfortable because they were designed for couples and families. I understand now how widows must feel, that they don't belong anywhere.

- I was especially fearful of being alone at night and vulnerable to intruders. I clung to those verses in Psalms and Proverbs that promised God's protection through the dark night. God was teaching me an invaluable lesson through these trials—that I needed to completely depend on Him, not on Ed.

- I wasn't the only one who was afraid. My husband is afraid of flying. He feared dying as much as I feared being a widow. The fears loomed largest in the dark night. It helped that Ed called me nightly to talk. We often cried together on the phone. He would say, "I don't want to be away from you, but I have to do my job. A lot of people are depending on me."

- In spite of the wedding ring he wears, during my husband's travels he has had women knock on his door in the middle of the night. We both feel angry and violated by that lack of respect. I feel torn between being there for my husband and fulfilling my responsibilities at home.

- I frequently mediated between Ed and our children because Ed was not there all week to observe daily events. He couldn't make decisions without sufficient information. I was constantly filling Ed in. "Always being in the middle" seemed to be the theme of my life.

- My son, Erik, enjoyed being man of the house in his father's absence. We are very close—so close that when Erik went away to college last year, I mourned for him. Ed's travels without my son at home seemed unbearable.

- Our daughter has struggled too. In the same manner that I missed my husband when he was away, she needed the stability of her father's presence.

THE POSITIVE SIDE

- Ed consistently worked at showing the children that he was thinking about them while he was away. When he was in town, he was a very involved father and attended all the children's activities.
- Our church family was a great comfort through those stressful years. I attended an informal moms' group on Tuesday mornings for years. I needed the adult contact.
- Ed's parents were my support system. They looked after us when Ed was traveling; in fact, we often stayed with them.
- Sometimes grandparents or friends kept our children so that I could go along with Ed on trips to places such as Japan, Singapore, and Europe. It was scary to be in a foreign country, but I was thrilled to be with my husband. Once I flew cross-country to surprise Ed at a dinner given in his honor.
- Ed and I are committed to meeting each other's needs. For example, Ed comes home to relieve me and care for me. And I try to prepare a relaxed environment in which he can unwind after his long, exhausting trips.
- I need to view myself as a responsible participant instead of a victim. I have learned to control my reactions when Ed tells me about his upcoming travel plans. When Ed became president of the company, his travel increased even more. He avoided telling me about his trips in advance because I would get so upset anticipating his departure that we could not enjoy the time we did have. Now we sit down and plan our calendars together, coordinating his trips and our family's schedule of activities at home.
- During school vacations we frequently took family trips so that our children could share in the advantages of the travel lifestyle. This was our life—we needed to make the most of it.

An outsider would probably advise a quick remedy to our struggles—that Ed find a job without travel. But my husband is in a sales profession that is never local in today's markets. We are involved in a family business, and Ed loves his work. At one point, he did take a desk job and stopped traveling for two years, but he was miserable.

He missed his contact with people. Any wife knows that it is better to live with a man who is happy in his work, no matter the challenges, than a man who is unhappy in his job.

Next year our daughter will be going to college, and we will experience the empty nest differently than our friends have. I do not dread it. Yes, I will miss my children, but I look forward to traveling again with my husband. We will simply include college campuses in our travels! Ed has already been visiting our son at college this past year, and I can't wait to go with him. The future looks bright as we reflect on our survival through some difficult years.

Epilogue

Ed was diagnosed with coronary artery disease and underwent an angioplasty. He and Charilyn have radically changed their lifestyle, including decreased travel, to care for Ed's health.

Disconnectedness
Anonymous

I am now on the other side of the travel challenge. Our son is in college and our daughter graduates from high school this year. As a salesman, my husband, Tim, traveled every week throughout their childhood. We handled things in a way that seemed right at the time, but now, with twenty years of hindsight, we see the mistakes we made. I hope that telling our story will help someone else who is starting on this path.

The Negative Side

- I did not want to be the ogre adding more demands to Tim's stressful schedule. By doing it all myself I thought I was helping, but now I realize that I was a hindrance. I wish I had told Tim that we needed him. I wish that I had urged him to *listen* to me.
- Tim and I talked every night on the phone but he didn't always

speak with the children, and now he wishes he had. Relayed messages were not the same. Our children needed that consistent contact with their father. A pattern of increasing disconnectedness developed that cannot be repaired now. It is a tragic feeling for parents to know that we can't get the past back.

- Girls need their mothers as role models but receive their esteem as women from their fathers. Our daughter, Ellen, has not fared well. She admits she does not have a good relationship with her dad; she doesn't feel special to him. Ellen says she doesn't know her dad well enough to trust him. Since I was with the children all week, when I got upset with them, they were unaffected. When Tim would legitimately become upset with them, Ellen became frightened. There was not sufficient context for her fearful reaction. Sometimes he would react quickly without knowing the background. I was often in the middle, trying to fill Tim in on the week's events. I tried to mediate apologies. It was a role with too much responsibility.

- Because of my nature and upbringing, I did not seek comfort in outside sources. Since childhood I was accustomed to being self-dependent. I couldn't count on others. I even struggled in my spiritual journey to learn to depend on God.

THE POSITIVE SIDE

- Tim received his esteem and affirmation from job success. He loves the children and me very much. He's been committed to our family, providing well for us. He and I both came from families in which the mothers were in charge, so that pattern seemed normal to us.

- Tim wholeheartedly supported my desire to be a full-time mother, providing a loving and secure homelife. We did enjoy a happy home environment.

- My teens and I have a close relationship. I've enjoyed being a full-time mom, participating in all their activities, being their cheerleader. As the children grew older and I worked part-time, I made sure that I was always home when they were. Teenagers need as much, or more, support and time with their parents as younger children.

- We had wonderful times as a family on the weekends, enjoying the latest recreational activities.

- Being realistic about our situation, we made financial sacrifices to place our children in a private Christian high school. Because of Tim's weekly absence, we felt our children needed that extra layer of protection from the influences of today's society.

- Our son missed his father but enjoyed being the man of the house. Boys receive their esteem as men from their mothers but need their fathers as role models. Our son is confident and feels good about himself. He didn't see Tim's absence as a loss; it was our normal life.

- We have supported our children 100 percent in whatever their interests were, no matter how uncomfortable for us. For example, we have sat on the floor with them and listened to music that we would never choose to hear. We have spent time in stables with horses. We have researched a wide range of topics. We have cheered them on in many activities that would not have been our personal choice. Our children once quipped, "We had no reason to rebel. We couldn't find anything that Mom and Dad would not support!"

- One very healthy thing we did was to openly discuss our struggles. We told the truth and had no secrets. We had problems, but we talked about them as a family. A mother wants to protect her children and hide pain from them, but children need to see their parents work through difficult situations so they can learn how to conquer their own pain and struggles as adults.

- We spent time nourishing our marriage relationship. Tim and I enjoyed each other's company. We took trips alone together throughout the year. When time was limited, we took trips on long weekends. When money was tight, we went camping; those are some of our most treasured memories.

- When I was lonely during Tim's absences, extended family was a great support. Church activities kept me busy. But I usually turned inward for strength.

- Being an introvert, I did not mind the quiet nights alone after the children were in bed. I enjoyed reading and studying and watching educational television. I love to learn. I think it is the wife's responsibility to plan the constructive use of her own time, to continue to grow and learn.

I may be on the other side of the travel life, but the challenges are not over. For these past twenty-five years, my husband and I have often talked about this empty nest/retirement stage of life we are now beginning. We planned for it to be "my turn." We dreamed about becoming innkeepers, working together and enjoying each other's company. It was my hope for the future during those difficult years of being alone.

But my husband has been diagnosed with a serious illness, one that could be terminal. Tim has been home this past year, learning that he didn't know his children the way he thought he did. We see now that we do not have forever. Looking back, would we have done things differently? Of course we would have.

THIRTY-FIVE YEARS WITH A TRAVELING HUSBAND
BY ELLEN TRIMBULL

Raising babies, raising teenagers, military life, and international travel have all been part of my thirty-five years of marriage to a traveling husband.

As a business manager, there has been nothing routine about Al's travel in terms of timing and duration. Together we set his career goals and decided upon the position he accepted. From the beginning we realized travel would be part of his job. We have viewed his travel as both a positive (broadening and enriching) and a negative (having him away) duty of his employment. It was helpful to have made this decision together and to understand its implications before we had children.

Especially when the children were young, my husband had no control over his travel. As a corporate insurance manager for a Fortune 500 company, he had to be prepared to leave immediately and stay as long as needed whenever there was a major insurance problem within their worldwide facilities. To free Al to do what was necessary to succeed in this position, we decided I would not work outside the home but rather be on full-time duty at the home front. His success depended upon my success and vice versa. Our income was perceived to be just that—*our* income.

I have always prepared our household budget, paid the bills, and made almost all financial decisions pertaining to household matters. Recently I have become the family investment manager, as well. Marriage is a partnership where job responsibilities are mutually decided and mutually respected.

With God's help, I have learned to be independent, flexible, and adjustable. After a while I could cope with, and handle, a lot more situations than I initially thought I could.

After the children were away at college, and at my husband's urging, I cleared my schedule to allow for trips with him. Often Al arranged a few days of vacation, and sometimes one of our daughters would come with us. When on a trip with him, breakfasts and dinners together are almost always possibilities, lunches usually are not. During the day there is plenty to see and do on my own, as well as needlework, writing, and reading that can be pursued in the hotel room.

Through the years, it was a help to me that Al and I agreed in advance we would not wait for phone calls. If something came up and I needed or wanted to be away, my husband understood. If my husband could not get to a phone at a reasonable hour, I understood. This eliminated many hard feelings, needless worry, or missed spur-of-the-moment invitations for me.

In our case, travel has brought an added dimension to our lives. Granted, it may have been easier in the early days because we had two daughters. Al's worst travel-related problem was the work that piled up at the office during his absence, putting demands on the time he would prefer to use catching up with family and home. It is easier to balance his traveling, career, family life, and spiritual walk now that the children are grown.

Many Scriptures have comforted and inspired me, including Micah 6:8, which says, "He has showed you, O man, what is good. And what does the Lord require of you? To act justly and to love mercy and to walk humbly with your God."

STRATEGY

Experience has seasoned the following tips from these veterans of the travel lifestyle.

For Husbands and Wives

- Trust in the Lord and know what you believe. This will be your foundation in a crisis.
- Do not entertain thoughts about divorce. Be committed to your marriage.
- Together pray about, and oversee, your children's educational and spiritual environment. They should be in a place where they can thrive.
- Establish an easy-to-locate file containing important household information including bank account numbers, phone numbers, and addresses of insurance and investment companies.
- Maintain a repair fund to cover those breakdowns that occur when the husband is away.
- Secure a spare key somewhere, or with someone, against the possibility of locking yourself out of the home or car.
- Accept that unpredictability is the major characteristic of the travel lifestyle. Focus on what is consistent in your life and be flexible with the areas outside of your control.
- Plan and dream together. Help each other accomplish goals.

For the Traveler

- Treat your wife as your "most important customer." Wine her, dine her, bring her flowers, and show that you cherish her.

- Listen to your wife. Help find solutions to her concerns.
- Take work with you to do on the plane or in the hotel room. Use the phone for business so your desk at the office will not be piled with projects when you return, causing you to miss additional time with your family.
- Use the phone to talk your wife through bookkeeping tasks, computer problems, or similar challenges. Talk your children through homework assignments.
- Provide protection for your family, such as a home alarm system, a car alarm, or a watchdog.
- Invest in a cellular phone so your wife can reach someone quickly if necessary while she and the children are away from home.
- Rest, exercise, eat well, and maintain your spiritual life so you can step right back into the family upon your return. When home, be an active part of the family, spending quantity and quality time with your wife and children. Resist the temptation to be "too tired."
- Develop common interests and hobbies with your wife and children.
- Refresh your wife—who has been "on" the whole time you were away—with some uninterrupted moments for a nap, a bubble bath, or a special outing.
- Take advantage of frequent-flyer programs to take family vacations.

For the Fort Soldier

- Don't "do it all." Allow your husband to hold his God-ordained place as head of the household.
- Encourage your husband and your children to have a genuine relationship of their own. Do not be their "middle man."
- Don't compare your life with others' lives. Keep your perspective; situations change and this stage in your life will soon move into something new. Find creative solutions to your challenges.
- Put up a map to track Dad's travels.
- Maintain a healthy diet, regular exercise, and get ample rest. Fa-

tigue is a major cause of depression and impatience.

- Organize your time. Find comfort in setting a schedule. Make it, keep it, adjust it—but don't serve it.
- Reduce your work load by organizing and decluttering the home.
- Train your children to help with household chores. It will lighten your load, help the children to be active participants in the family, and prepare them to care for their own homes in the future.
- Do something fun and relaxing with the children. Include lots of eye contact, playtime, laughter, and hugs.
- Understand your temperament, strengths, weaknesses, and special needs. Use your strong points, and cultivate support for the weaker areas.
- Find your identity outside your spouse. You are responsible for your own happiness.
- Be involved in your husband's job, available to be his sounding board, and listen to his plans.
- Spend time reading literature that encourages your role as a wife, mother, and homemaker. Include books and articles about favorite hobbies and interests. Avoid the trap of romance novels that ultimately cause you to be discontented with your own marriage. Concentrate on writings that build your relationship with your husband.
- When you see a way to do something special for someone else, do it.
- Seek healthy friendships with people you can trust. Healthy relationships are not exclusive, rescuing, testing, jealous, always there, smothering, or competitive.
- Realize children need extra tender loving care, more protection, and more supervision from the parent who holds down the fort. Possibly the greatest responsibility for you as a fort soldier is to be the anchor for your children, being totally available to them.
- Life does not stop when your husband is away. Each day brings a myriad of decisions you are quite capable of making and carrying out on your own. You are not helpless. If you make a poor decision, learn from the experience and put it behind you.

For the Church and Others

- Care for the children so the wife can accompany her husband on a trip.
- Offer Bible studies with programs for the children.
- Get together for tea or coffee, for prayer and encouragement.

CHAPTER SIXTEEN

Manning the Fort

I lift up my eyes to the hills—where does my help come from? My help comes from the Lord, the Maker of heaven and earth. He will not let your foot slip—he who watches over you will not slumber; indeed, he who watches over Israel will neither slumber nor sleep. The Lord watches over you—the Lord is your shade at your right hand; the sun will not harm you by day, nor the moon by night. The Lord will keep you from all harm—He will watch over your life; the Lord will watch over your coming and going both now and forevermore.

—*PSALM 121*

C AN WE HAVE HEALTHY FAMILIES AND A TRAVELING SPOUSE? The answer is a resounding YES! But it requires much hard work. What does a healthy family look like? Research has identified the following characteristics of healthy families:

- There is open communication and good listening skills in operation. There are no family secrets.
- There is unconditional love and commitment evident among family members.
- They trust each other.
- There exists a genuine appreciation and affection for one another.
- They respect one another and pass on solid values to the younger.
- They share responsibility for the family and are supportive of one another.
- They maintain a spiritual focus.
- They enjoy special family times and practice family traditions.
- They cultivate skills for dealing effectively with stress and crisis.

Healthy families are not those who enjoy an ideal, problem-free lifestyle. The travel lifestyle is difficult for all families. But our lifestyle is not the deciding factor—how we handle our challenge is what makes the difference. This is the ultimate balancing act.

GOD'S SURVIVAL GUIDE
IS TRAVEL BIBLICAL?

Have our culture's demands collided with our biblical values? Can separating, uprooting, and relocating families be part of God's plan? Our immediate reaction (at least mine) is *no*. Families come first, children come first—isn't this what God intended?

Some would label this cultural view "worshiping the family over worshiping God." Is the comfort and happiness of families a biblical priority? Look at the lives of Abraham, Moses, Noah, Ruth, Jonah, Jesus, His disciples, and Paul.

God called them to travel to strange places, endure uncomfortable journeys, make great sacrifices, uproot their lives in the face of ridicule from those around them, suffer imprisonment, even face death. God called His people to follow Him at all cost. That call remains constant regardless of culture, and we are called to do the same. The big question is not "Do we travel?" The big question is "Are we following God's calling or our own desires?"

In a society where throw-away relationships are becoming the norm, "fort soldiers" are committed to their families and spouses no matter how difficult their circumstances. In a society where spouses end marriages because their needs are not being met, fort soldiers put others' needs before their own, trusting God's care for themselves. Pushed to the limit, fort soldiers do not survive without an authentic, dependent relationship with their Lord. There can be no pretense. There is no where else to run. God is their fortress.

Fort soldiers are honest with God, their families, and themselves. In the uncomfortable, painful, and lonely job of holding down the fort, God refines us and teaches us perseverance. Though lonely, we know we are not alone. God holds us with arms that never let go. An intimate relationship with Him is the result of the travel challenge. What could be more biblical?

CULTIVATING YOUR SPIRITUAL LIFE

- Do not neglect your spiritual life. If your schedule is not conducive to early morning Bible reading and prayer, carve the time out at noon or in the evening. Regular prayer and Bible study will prove to be your strength in every aspect of your life and family.
- Prayer is the tie between God and separated spouses. Pray for one another and for each child every day, whether you are together or in separate parts of the world.
- Depend completely on God. Be rooted in scriptural truth. Healthy relationships are based on Jesus Christ as Savior as opposed to an unhealthy dependence on your mate.
- The key to committed marriages is reliance on God's strength with a focus on intact families over personal comfort.
- Be regularly involved in a Bible-believing church. Even the spouse on the road can attend a church in the town where he is visiting.
- Whether at home or on the road, nourish your spiritual life through Christian books, Christian radio, teaching tapes, magazines, and uplifting praise music.
- Exercise consistent memorization of life-saving Bible verses. Below is a sampling of verses fellow fort soldiers have committed to life and heart.

PROMISES OF COMFORT FROM THE PSALMS

When we feel abandoned . . .

> But you, O God, do see trouble and grief;
> you consider it to take it in hand.
> The victim commits himself to you;
> you are the helper of the fatherless. —Psalm 10:14

> I will not take my love from him,
> nor will I ever betray my faithfulness. —Psalm 89:33

When we know despair and hopelessness . . .

> Turn your ear to me,
> come quickly to my rescue;
> be my rock of refuge,
> a strong fortress to save me.
> Since you are my rock and my fortress,
> for the sake of your name lead and guide me. —Psalm 31:2–3

> The salvation of the righteous comes from the Lord;
> he is their stronghold in time of trouble.
> The Lord helps them and delivers them;
> he delivers them from the wicked and saves them,
> because they take refuge in him. —Psalm 37:39–40

When we feel like we are slipping . . .

> In the day of my trouble I will call to you,
> for you will answer me. —Psalm 86:7

> When I said, "My foot is slipping,"
> your love, O Lord, supported me.
> When anxiety was great within me,
> your consolation brought joy to my soul. —Psalm 94:18–19

When we are exhausted . . .

> The Lord is my shepherd, I shall lack nothing.
> He makes me to lie down in green pastures,
> he leads me beside quiet waters,
> he restores my soul. —Psalm 23:1–3

> My soul finds rest in God alone;
> my salvation comes from him.
> He alone is my rock and my salvation;
> he is my fortress, I will never be shaken. —Psalm 62:1–2

When we feel weak . . .

> Whom have I in heaven but you?

And being with you, I desire nothing on earth.
My flesh and my heart may fail,
but God is the strength of my heart
and my portion forever. —Psalm 73:25–26

When my spirit grows faint within me,
it is you who know my way. —Psalm 142:3

When we are depressed and feel like we are drowning . . .

May your unfailing love be my comfort,
according to your promise to your servant.
Let your compassion come to me that I may live,
for your law is my delight. —Psalm 119:76–77

Reach down your hand from on high;
deliver me and rescue me. —Psalm 144:7

When we feel our world is falling apart . . .

You have made known to me the path of life;
you will fill me with joy in your presence,
with eternal pleasures at your right hand. —Psalm 16:11

God is our refuge and strength,
an ever-present help in trouble.
Therefore we will not fear,
though the earth give way
and the mountains fall into the heart of the sea. . . .
The Lord Almighty is with us. —Psalm 46:1–2, 7

When we lose our purpose . . .

I will praise the Lord who counsels me;
even at night my heart instructs me. —Psalm 16:7

I will instruct you and teach you
in the way you should go. —Psalm 32:8

When we are afraid at night . . .

I will lie down and sleep in peace,

for You alone, O Lord,
make me dwell in safety. —Psalm 4:8

He will cover you with his feathers,
and under his wings you will find refuge;
his faithfulness will be your shield and rampart.
You will not fear the terror of night. . . .
If you make the Most High your dwelling—
even the Lord, who is my refuge—
then no harm will befall you,
no disaster will come near your tent.
For he will command His angels concerning you
to guard you in all your ways. —Psalm 91:4–5, 9–11

When we feel left behind . . .

Trust in him at all times, O people;
pour out your hearts to him,
for God is our refuge. —Psalm 62:8

May your unfailing love be my comfort,
according to your promise to your servant. —Psalm 119:76

When travel and distance overwhelm us . . .

I am confident of this:
I will see the goodness of the Lord
in the land of the living.
Wait for the Lord;
be strong and take heart
and wait for the Lord. —Psalm 27:13–14

If I rise on the wings of the dawn,
if I settle on the far side of the sea,
even there your hand will guide me,
your right hand will hold me fast. —Psalm 139:9–10

PeggySue's Epilogue

"Call to me and I will answer you and show you great and unsearchable things you do not know." I sought the Lord, and he answered me; he delivered me from all my fears.

Those who look to him are radiant; their faces are never covered with shame.

—*JEREMIAH 33:3; PSALM 34:4–5*

THIS HAD BEEN THE HARDEST YEAR OF OUR MARRIAGE. I thought we were doing better. Until today.

Keith had been summoned to jury duty and had already arranged the time off from work. All week he had said if he were not selected, he would be home early to have a few hours with me. I believed him.

Last week Keith was away on business again. I spent the days unpacking from a camping trip, canning fruit from our trees, and going to the children's music lessons. During the same week, the kitchen drawers fell apart, mice invaded the whole house (one was barricaded in our bedroom closet), the van still needed work, and the baby turned two.

I was exhausted. I missed my husband, my best friend. The children missed their dad. The brief interruption caused by jury duty seemed God's gift of time together for us. Even if Keith was selected, he would be home earlier than usual because he would not have to commute.

The court case was dismissed and Keith was home at 10:00 A.M. The children and I were excited; he was distracted and tense. If he went to the office he could get a half-day's work done. Keith stayed home long enough to listen to a twenty-minute Christian radio broadcast about commitment to family, then said he was going to the office. After all, he had been away for a week.

"You've been away from us for a week too," I said.

"You have plans for the day," he justified.

"Nothing I couldn't cancel," I said. "Being with you is far more important."

"I have a lot of work to get done on the budgets. What do you think?" he asked.

"You don't want to know," I replied, hoping he did. The air was tense. As one of our daughters practiced her violin, strains of "Faded Love" floated out to us in the living room. *Is this what we've come to? I wondered. Doesn't he hear it?*

"Okay," he said. "I'll see you tonight." And he drove away.

I was so disappointed. I went up to my room so the children wouldn't see me cry. Over the months my emotions had grown numb. I hadn't been able to cry for longer than I could remember. But now I sobbed. I spent my life waiting for Keith, for any scrap of time he could toss my way. The job cut into my time with Keith; business trips away took my evenings and weekends with him. And I was supposed to be patient and understand. But I didn't understand anymore. I was weary of being a single parent. I hurt each time the pressures of the job put me in second place in my husband's heart.

Fiery pain flamed through my shoulder and down my right arm again. Three doctors over the past two years had diagnosed a stress-related condition that threatened the use of the arm. Keith and I have enjoyed one of the best husband-and-wife relationships I've ever seen, but this past six months we'd had some real fights. Each argument had the same theme. I was drowning. I don't hide my feelings, I talk. But Keith stopped listening. Eight months earlier a promotion translated into greater overload at work. I was happy to see him achieve his career goals, and I did my best to support him. But the cost of his heavy responsibilities and absences was paid by our family. There was little left in him to give to us. All our personal goals and dreams sat withering on the dusty "someday" shelf. Depression intensified my physical struggles.

After my emotions were spent, I went back downstairs to finish putting the dinner recipe together. The children heard Keith's key in the lock before I did. Taking my hand, he led me back to the couch.

"I knew things weren't right," Keith said. "So I pulled off the road and prayed. I wanted to be sure I was making the right decision."

"You probably came home because you knew I was angry and hurt," I responded. "I don't want you home because I've manipulated you. I can't make you want to be with me, I just wish you did."

"That's one of the things I prayed about," he said. "I made sure I wasn't coming home because of pressure from you. Keeping my priorities straight is hard. At least this time I caught it. Just be patient with me; don't give up on me."

"We've always had a standard of being there for one another," I reminded him. "Each time that gets violated, I'm the one who gets hurt. I haven't given up on you, but I can't count on you either."

"I'm sorry," Keith replied. "Please forgive me. I'm working on it. Today is a gift from God. I've already thrown part of it away. I want to be a good steward with the rest of it."

During that same summer, the Lord provided an opportunity for me to accompany Keith on a business trip to the East Coast. Leaving my children with friends for five days was the hardest thing I've ever done.

Having said good-bye to the children, I boarded the plane with the same enthusiasm I'd had going in for bunion surgery. My heart was torn between feeling I needed to be with my children and knowing how much Keith wanted me along on this trip. It occurred to me that Keith must feel just as torn each time he needs to leave his family in order to support us through his employment.

I was fascinated with how comfortably Keith moves through the world of airports, shuttles, rental cars, hotels, and restaurants. He moves through the process as easily as I move through my home, knowing where to find everything and how it all should work. Even on the road, Keith's responsibilities to his family and his office continue to need his constant attention. Settled in at our hotel, we phoned to check in with the children each day.

"Yes, Josiah," Keith spoke through the receiver, "for this week, Jennifer is your boss. You must do what she says until we get back. I love you, son. We'll be home soon."

Keith also checked in at the office daily. His phone calls to the office kept shipments and programs from being delayed.

"What's going on?" he'd ask his staff.

After a pause, "What did Jim say?"

Another pause. "Okay, pass me through to Armando."

Silence.

"Mando, where's my 35's? You have blanks coming in."

Another pause to listen.

"Put me on with Jim." And so the phone calls would go as Keith juggled work in California from Virginia.

The convention went well, and I enjoyed seeing a new part of the country, eating at nice restaurants, and spending time with Keith in between his meetings and presentations. But the biggest advantage was that glimpse into Keith's world.

For the next six months, Keith did his best for his family and his company, while I did my best to support him and care for the children while he traveled. Yet we prayed the Lord would eventually release Keith to a job that would allow him to be home more.

One last major trial stood between us and the miracle God planned for our family. In September I had a bouquet of flowers delivered to Keith's office. The attached note read, "Congratulations." We were thrilled to be expecting our sixth child. Three months into the pregnancy, I was bedridden with severe nausea and migraines complicated with pneumonia. Keith was slated to fly overseas for three weeks. The timing could not have been worse. He felt choosing to stay home might cost him his job.

After much prayer and agonizing, Keith told his boss he could not go. Someone else made the trip, and the Lord confirmed Keith had made the right decision.

Within a few months, a job opened with his biggest customer.

Keith's résumé dovetailed with the job description perfectly. Keith's travel would be reduced from frequent to rare. Our whole family flew to Indiana to see if we liked the area. In the state only twenty-four hours, we found our dream home.

After much prayer, Keith accepted the new job. Thanks to the Lord, we've traded earthquakes for tornado watches, traffic jams for train crossings, and Keith's ninety-minute commute for a twenty-minute drive to work. I praise the Lord each time Keith comes home for lunch, goes fishing with the children, does an evening math lesson with them, and plays tag or builds snowmen on the front lawn. I appreciate the additional time Keith has with our family.

Keith still must guard his priorities, manage his time wisely, and cope with life's stresses. The van still breaks down, the yard still needs maintenance, and the dishwasher still gives us fits. But it was worth the move because Keith is home more, and we have greater opportunity to meet life's challenges together.

Though Keith does catch a flight once in a while, we feel he has come home. God has answered our prayers in a unique way as only He could do.

Mary Ann's Epilogue

Know that the Lord has set apart the godly for himself;
the Lord will hear when I call to him.

—PSALM 4:3

WONDERS COME IN DIFFERENT FORMS. The miracle we most fervently pray for is that God will change our circumstances. In control of every detail that touches our lives, He is capable of accomplishing any miracle.

But often God chooses to do a greater miracle. He carries us through the circumstances that He does not change. Whether we experience the death of a loved one, a painful divorce, severe illness, rebellious children, the travel lifestyle, or a host of other heartbreaking human trials, our loving Father holds us. Our survival through the fire is the ultimate miracle—the miracle that converts our spiritual life to gold and leads us home.

PeggySue and I have each experienced God's miracles in our lives this past year—very different miracles. God provided PeggySue's family with a dream home in Indiana and a dream job for Keith with rare travel. They have never been happier, enjoying an ideal family lifestyle.

At the same time, God turned up the flame on my family's life. I've seen the wonder of His sustaining hand through our most difficult year of marriage. The month that PeggySue moved, John merged his company with another company on the East Coast. He became immersed in high-pressure corporate life that required him to travel weekly. We

189

were also involved in lawsuits that took an emotional toll. I didn't just feel left behind; I *was* left behind.

John and I were each stretched to the limit. John continued to live on Eastern time even when he was home in California. He would go to the office at 4:00 A.M. and fall asleep by 8:30 P.M. when I was trying to put the children to bed. His schedule was tight and unpredictable. I felt that I could rarely count on him.

Caring for our family was all I could manage. I gave up outside interests and activities, such as writing and teaching music. Luncheons for friends ended. I was too exhausted to organize them. PeggySue, one of the few friends who shared my situation, was gone. My long-time single girlfriend, who provided late-night chats, married and was unavailable. God was stripping away all my support systems.

Most traumatic was the death of my beloved father. He entered the hospital a few weeks before Christmas for an angiogram, had emergency heart surgery, and didn't survive. Because John was traveling, I flew to Los Angeles with two of my children for the surgery, leaving my teenager with good friends. John and my eldest met us in Los Angeles later. It was the most painful week of my life. I lived in a fog of deep grief for months. The message was clear: God was my ultimate support. God may send angels along the way, but He alone is our strength.

Practical survival methods changed. Recent burglaries in our area prompted us to install an alarm system. No different from wearing seat belts in the car, that protection system insures me a good night's sleep when John is absent, when I need it most.

Our three active children are getting older and more challenging. The teen years usher in numerous outside activities. Because of time differences, we often miss Dad's daily phone calls while we are at school functions or other activities. We try to videotape special events that John misses.

On a positive note, we do have the opportunity to travel with John now that our children are older. Finances are never a concern. We remain adamant about having family recovery time on the weekend.

John simply refuses to travel then. We have curtailed most church activities.

I realize we are living through a transition period, and we've lived through them before. Sixteen years ago John took a new position at a hospital in another part of the state. We lived apart for the summer while I sold the house and wrapped up loose ends. For a year after we moved, I traveled back to our former home two days a week, negotiating airports comfortably. Life was challenging and exciting as I finished my doctoral research at the hospital where I worked, completing courses, exams, giving recitals, and graduating. Our first child was born a year later. Until recently I had honestly forgotten that I was once the traveling spouse, as well as a workaholic.

I have lived on both sides of the travel lifestyle. It is not easy for anyone. John and I remain committed to supporting each other, no matter the cost. God holds us on both sides and refines our faith in His purpose. "But now, this is what the Lord says. . . . 'Fear not, for I have redeemed you; I have called you by name; you are mine. When you pass through the waters, I will be with you; and when you pass through the rivers, they will not sweep over you. When you walk through the fire, you will not be burned; the flames will not set you ablaze. For I am the Lord, your God, the Holy One of Israel, your Savior' " (Isa. 43:1–3).

Thank you for selecting a book from
BETHANY HOUSE PUBLISHERS

Bethany House Publishers is a ministry of Bethany Fellowship
International, an interdenominational, nonprofit organization
committed to spreading the Good News of Jesus Christ around
the world through evangelism, church planting, literature
distribution, and care for those in need. Missionary training is
offered through Bethany College of Missions.

Bethany Fellowship International is a member of the National
Association of Evangelicals and subscribes to its statement of
faith. If you would like further information, please contact:

Bethany Fellowship International
6820 Auto Club Road
Minneapolis, MN 55438 USA